Designing Competence-Based Training

Second Edition

SHIRLEY FLETCHER

**KOGAN
PAGE**

London • Stirling (USA)

To Mum and Dad

First published in 1991
Reprinted 1995
This second edition published 1997

Apart from any fair dealing for the purposes of research or private study, or criticism or review, as permitted under the Copyright, Designs and Patents Act, 1988, this publication may only be reproduced, stored or transmitted, in any form or by any means, with the prior permission in writing of the publishers, or in the case of reprographic reproduction in accordance with the terms of licences issued by the Copyright Licensing Agency. Enquiries concerning reproduction outside those terms should be sent to the publishers at the undermentioned address:

Kogan Page Limited
120 Pentonville Road
London N1 9JN
and
22883 Quicksilver Drive
Stirling, VA 20166, USA

© Shirley Fletcher, 1991, 1995, 1997

British Library Cataloguing in Publication Data

A CIP record for this book is available from the British Library.

ISBN 0 7494 2196 7

Typeset by Saxon Printing Ltd, Derby
Printed and bound in Great Britain by Biddles Ltd, Guildford

Designing
Competence-Based
Training

The Kogan Page Practical Trainer Series
Series Editor: Roger Buckley

'Excellent and challenging' The Learning World, BBC World Service
'Jargon-free and straightforward... sound advice' Personnel Management
'Clear, informative, very practically oriented' The Training Officer

Contents

Series Editor's Foreword

Organizations get things done when people do their jobs effectively. To make this happen they need to be well trained. A number of people are likely to be involved in this training by identifying the needs of the organization and of the individual, by selecting or designing appropriate training to meet those needs, by delivering it and by assessing how effective it was. It is not only 'professional' or full-time trainers who are involved in this process: personnel managers, line managers, supervisors and job holders are all likely to have a part to play.

This series has been written for all those who get involved with training in some way or another, whether they are senior personnel managers trying to link the goals of the organization with training needs or job holders who have been given responsibility for training newcomers. Therefore, the series is essentially a practical one which focuses on specific aspects of the training function. This is not to say that the theoretical underpinnings of the practical aspects of training are unimportant. Anyone seriously interested in training is strongly encouraged to look beyond 'what to do' and 'how to do it' and to delve into the areas of why things are done in a particular way.

The authors have been selected because they have considerable practical experience. All have shared, at some time, the same difficulties, frustrations and satisfactions of being involved in training and are now in a position to share with others some helpful and practical guidelines.

In this new edition Shirley Fletcher examines the design of training programmes based on standards of occupational competence. This approach aims at developing a competent workforce by focusing on the establishment of standards by which to measure competence in the workplace. It is of value not only to organizations that want to link their training with national standards but those who may wish to approach their training from a different perspective.

The implications for the trainer include a move away from training programmes based on task analysis to programmes based on functional analysis. This concentrates on identifying the purpose of the organization and its occupational roles together with the standards expected of individual job holders. The emphasis on individual performance has to take into account learning styles, a wider range of learning strategies and more individualized learning programmes.

ROGER BUCKLEY

Preface

This book is directed at trainers who have some experience of training design, but particularly at those who want to take a fresh approach and move away from traditional forms of training and development. It outlines the principles and practice involved in designing training based on explicit standards of competent performance.

New trends in competence-based standards, assessment and training have increased the focus on learner-centred learning. As use of new competence-based systems expands, training professionals will need to respond quickly and effectively to the increased involvement of learners in their own learning process. Trainers will find themselves working in a training and development context in which there will be:

- a modular structure of training
- greater access to and demand for learning and assessment
- greater links between education and training
- a more focused approach to training design
- wider and broader demands on the trainer.

This presents new challenges for trainers in all working contexts. New trends will require that training staff become involved in all aspects of the training cycle and not simply in delivery. It also opens up new and exciting arenas in which trainers can innovate and explore new methods of training delivery.

A key to the new form of training design is *flexibility*. Traditional start and finish dates for courses will need to be replaced by delivery schedules that meet individual and group needs; methods of delivery will need to be broadened to allow for all learning styles; and direct access to assessment will have to be made available.

When designing competence-based training, therefore, the trainer is adopting an *individualized, flexible* and *integrated* approach to the training function.

This book outlines the foundations on which competence-based training design must be built. It provides checklists, diagrams, charts and example material, including case studies from organizations currently involved in these developments.

Since first publication of this book, the Training and Development Lead Body has formally approved and published national standards for trainers, together with an NVQ Framework. (National Launch, 4 March 1992.) Revised standards are due in 1998.

Acknowledgements

All examples of UK national standards appear with the kind permission of the Industry Lead Body concerned.

The author would like to thank the following people for the time and effort they contributed to the preparation of case study material: Mike Holliday, Regional Manager, Cellar Service Function, Whitbread Beer Company; Mike Saunders, Training and Development Manager, British Telecom; Viv Taylor, Training and Development Manager, Boots plc.

I would also like to thank the many contacts in the following organizations for their help and support regarding the use of example materials: Chemical Industries Association; Hotel and Catering Training Company; National Forum for Management Education and Development; Clothing and Allied Products Industry Training Board; Training and Development Lead Body; Computing Services Industry Training Council; The Pensions Management Institute; National Retail Training Council; The Building Societies Lead Body; City and Guilds; Training, Enterprise and Education Directorate; Department of Employment; Scotvec; and Business and Technician Education Council.

Please note that all references in this book to NVQs (National Vocational Qualifications) apply also to SVQs (Scottish Vocational Qualifications) under common guidance and criteria.

1 What is Competence-Based Training?

▷	SUMMARY	◁

This chapter helps you to:
- Understand the basic foundations of competence-based training.
- Identify the importance of competence-based training for your organization.
- Consider the implications of competence-based systems for your role as a trainer.

Two Competence-Based Systems

The introduction of standards of occupational competence is changing the face of training and development in the UK, the USA and, increasingly, in other national HRD systems. Anyone with responsibility for the identification of training needs and/or the design, delivery and evaluation of training will need to understand and apply the concepts and operational principles of competence-based training.

There are two major types of competence-based system, each having its own conceptual base and characteristics. They are not totally incompatible, and by understanding both you can draw on the best and most applicable aspects to apply within your own context. The basis of both systems is outlined below and explored in more detail in Chapter 2.

The purpose of competence-based training is the development of a competent workforce. In UK terms, a competent workforce is comprised of individuals who can *consistently* perform work activities to the

1

standards required in employment over a *range* of contexts or conditions. In the USA, competencies are defined as 'not the tasks of the job, [but] what enable people to do the tasks'.

In the UK, *competence* reflects the *expectations of employment*, and focuses on *work roles* rather than *jobs*. In the USA, *competence* is *an underlying characteristic* of a person which results in *effective and/or superior performance* in a job.

These differences actually represent quite a divergence in conceptual thought – a divergence which can result in very different approaches to the development of standards ('competences' in the UK, 'competencies' in the USA), to the format in which final standards are presented, and to the application of those standards within training programmes.

Implications for Trainers

Misunderstandings about competence-based systems, and thus about competence based-training, usually arise from one of the following difficulties:

- A mistaken belief that new competence-based systems such as National Vocational Qualifications (NVQs) are systems of *training*, rather than of *assessment*.
- A difficulty with focusing on *outcomes* rather than processes or inputs.
- A mistaken belief that the actual process or methods of designing training will radically change.
- A mistaken belief that competence-based training means that the training role will be taken out of the hands of the trainer.

Training/Assessment

In the UK, within state-of-the-art developments, *outcome-based* standards of competence are incorporated into *units of competence*. These units combine, in various ways, to form National Vocational Qualifications (NVQs). It is important to understand that a unit of competence is a unit of *assessment and certification*. A number of training modules may be required for, or relate to, any one unit of competence.

Outcome/Input or Process

Any trainer experienced in the design of training programmes automatically thinks in terms of training objectives, together with the structure and content of programmes. Competence-based training also has objectives, structure and defined content. The key difference is really the starting point for design. Trainers now need to think more in terms of *required outputs* than desirable inputs.

In competence-based training, explicit, outcome-based standards are always used as the planning foundation.

Change in Process or Methods of Design

The methods of training delivery and the basic tools of training design do not radically change within a competence based system. Trainers will probably find that the range of options open to them increases as the opportunity to increase flexibility of training approach is presented. Trainers will be able to create new approaches to meet individual and group needs, building in practical assessments to a greater degree and innovating methods and processes to help individuals provide contributory evidence of their competence through the completion of training activities.

The Trainer Role

Competence-based systems do encourage everyone within an organization to take responsibility for training and development. For example, line managers take more of a coaching and development role and need to become more effective in identifying training needs. This does not mean, however, that the trainer becomes redundant! To the contrary, the trainer becomes more of a consultant and has the opportunity to work more closely with line managers and individuals in the identification of needs, design and delivery of training and in the evaluation of its effectiveness.

The Basic Foundation

The key difference between traditional and competence-based training lies in the basis on which the training cycle is operated. In a competence-based system, the basis must be explicit, measurable standards of performance which are outcome-based and reflect the actual expectations of performance in a work role.

The design of competence-based training is conducted along the lines illustrated in Figure 1.1. This model is explored in detail in the following chapters.

3

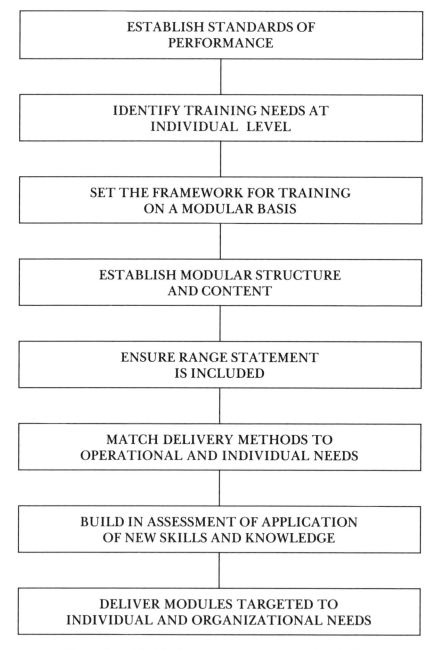

Figure 1.1 *Model of competence-based training design*

► REVIEW ◄

The purpose of competence-based training is the development of a competent workforce.

In a competence-based system, the basis of training design must be explicit and measurable standards of performance, which are outcome-based and reflect the actual expectations of performance in a work role.

There are many misunderstandings about competence-based systems, and thus about competence-based training. These usually arise from one of the following:

- a mistaken belief that all competence-based systems are systems of *training*, rather than systems of *assessment*;

- a difficulty with focusing on *outcomes* rather than processes or inputs;

- a mistaken belief that the actual process or methods of designing training will radically change;

- a mistaken belief that competence-based training means the training role will be taken out of the hands of the trainer.

2 Getting to Grips with Basics

▷	SUMMARY	◁

This chapter will help you with:
- understanding and using two major competence-based standards systems
- focusing on outcome-based systems
- considering the basic aspects of competence-based training
- learning about training and assessment related to public certification of competence
- considering the use of competence-based models within your own training context.

As with all competence-based activities, design of training starts with explicit standards of occupational competence.

NVQs: National Standards in the UK

Standards of occupational competence or competence-based standards, as they are usually known, are being developed across all occupations of all sectors of all industries. These standards differ from those traditionally used with training/learning programmes in several major respects.

The new standards are:

- outcome-based
- employment-led
- independent of any training or learning programme
- based on work roles rather than job descriptions

- independent of assessment method
- removed from time constraints and entry restrictions in respect of learning programmes.

These aspects of competence-based standards have significant implications for the processes of assessment. (This issue will be discussed in detail in Chapter 5.)

Outcome-based

The standards are presented in a format which reflects the expectations of performance in the workplace. They make explicit the expected products or *outcomes* of workplace performance.

Employment-led

In the UK, national competence-based standards are developed and agreed by commerce and industry. Development of standards is managed by *Industry Lead Bodies*. Final standards are agreed by consultation throughout the relevant industry.

These employment-led standards reflect a benchmark of competent performance across a specific sector of industry. The master plan is, of course, that all employers adopt these standards within their recruitment, selection, training, appraisal and manpower planning activities thus providing a common standard of workplace performance. The use of explicit standards, and of a unit-based system of assessment and accreditation, should also serve to raise the quality of workplace performance and the flexibility of training within commerce and industry.

Independent of Training or Learning Programmes

The standards do not belong to any one training programme or course of study (as has been the case with more traditional systems of learning and assessment for certification). *How* individuals learn, and their rate of progress, *are* issues for trainers, but not for the final outcome of work-related training – competent workplace performance. The standards can therefore be used on a flexible, learner-centred basis and incorporated into a wide variety of training programmes and courses, each using a wide variety of methods.

Independent of Assessment Method

If standards are independent of (specified) programmes of learning, then clearly they are also *independent of the assessment methods* used within specified programmes of learning. This issue is discussed in Chapter 5.

No Entry Restrictions or Time Constraints

The removal of a direct link to specified programmes is accompanied by removal of entry requirements for learning programmes and of time constraints on both learning and achievement of standards. Individuals therefore progress (within the workplace) towards competent performance at their own pace. We examine this issue in more depth in Chapter 5.

Work Roles not Job Descriptions

Competence-based standards are derived through a process of *functional analysis*: a top-down analytical approach which, at industry-sector level, begins with the *key purpose* of sector activity.

From the key purpose, a number of 'key work roles' are agreed. The analytical process continues until 'units of competence' are identified.

As the terminology suggests, this approach focuses on *functions* and not tasks. In its simplest form, the difference between these two concepts is:

- **Task** – the work activity to be completed.
- **Function** – the purpose of the work activity to be completed.

It is believed that the functional approach results in standards which reflect a broader concept of competence. This broader concept might take into account not simply the tasks that are undertaken, but the way in which tasks are organized within the work role, and the management of contingencies (Mansfield and Matthews, 1985).

The functional approach, then, requires a clear focus on the broad *work role* and not simply the job. Trainers should therefore avoid the use of job descriptions as the only or major basis for training design. Job descriptions, titles and contents vary drastically, both within and between industries. The same 'job' can have many different titles – and different jobs can have the same title. Job descriptions are also generally 'task-based'.

Given the confusion about job titles/job descriptions, therefore, a clearer common ground can be established by shifting the focus on to 'work roles' (across sectors and between jobs) rather than jobs alone.

This key point must be kept in mind when designing competence-based training. Much traditional training design has used the job description as its basis. With the new competence-based approach, training becomes, in effect, multidimensional – the trainer must learn to think in terms of work roles, and plan training which crosses traditional job barriers.

The NVQ Framework

Training and Qualifications

In the UK, the new system of qualifications based on competence-based standards leads to individuals achieving National Vocational Qualifications (NVQs). An NVQ is:

> A statement of competence relevant to employment. It is this statement which specifies the competence to be achieved . . . It is the basis from which assessment procedures, recording and certification are derived. (NCVQ 1988b)

To be accredited as a National Vocational Qualification, a qualification must be:

- based firmly on national standards required for performance in employment, and take proper account of future needs with particular regard to technology, markets and employment patterns;
- based on assessments of the outcomes of learning, specified independently of any particular mode, duration or location of learning;
- awarded on the basis of valid and reliable assessments made in such a way as to ensure that performance to the national standards can be achieved at work;
- free from barriers which restrict access and progression, and available to all those who are able to reach the required standards by whatever means;
- free from overt or covert discriminatory practices with regard to gender, age, race or creed and designed to pay due regard to the special needs of individuals. (NCVQ, 1995)

NVQs are comprised of units of competence, each unit being a unit of *assessment and certification*. This structure is illustrated in Figure 2.1. It is not linked to periods of study, only to achievement in a work role.

Credit Accumulation

Units of competence can relate to functions undertaken in more than one sector of industry. A holder of a unit in one sector may find that this unit has 'exchange value' in another. Obviously, the sectors in which exchange of units is possible must be related in some way. Examples might be the overlap between hotel and catering and tourism or between tourism and travel. As each sector of commerce

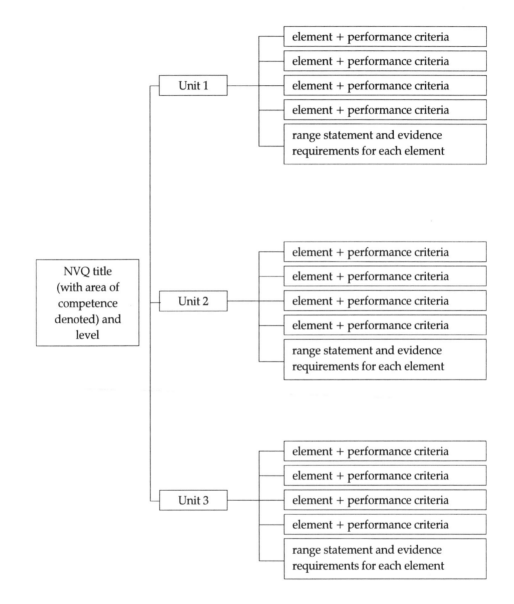

Figure 2.1 *NVQ structure*

and industry establishes and agrees units of competence so the exchange value of units between sectors is also established.

The entire UK assessment and certification system operates on a 'credit accumulation and transfer' basis. As individuals are successfully assessed against competence-based standards, they are able to achieve the units of competence relevant to their work role. This process is undertaken at the individual's own pace. 'Credits' can be accumulated over time, from different workplaces, and in different sectors.

Units of Competence

A unit of competence is:

> a primary sub-division of the competence needed to be achieved for the award of an NVQ, representing a discrete aspect of competence which may be recognised and certificated independently as a credit towards an award. Units are comprised of one or more elements of competence. (NCVQ, 1988a and 1995)

In short, a unit of competence represents an activity which can be undertaken by one individual, and which has real meaning in the workplace. It is a unit of *assessment and certification*, the smallest part of an award which can be separately certificated.

Units of competence are made up of 'competence-based standards'. The standards themselves consist of an *element of competence* and its related *performance criteria*, together with a *range statement* and, guidance on the types of evidence of performance required for successful assessment.

The development of standards, and their use in programme design, will be discussed in the next chapter. For the present, however, it might be helpful to see an example unit (pages 12–13).

Quality Control

New systems of assessment and accreditation, in which competence-based standards form the foundation stones, lead to:

- flexibility in assessment
- flexibility of training/learning programmes
- removal of time limits on learning and assessment
- a common standard of workplace performance.

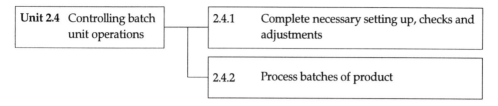

| Unit 2.4 Controlling batch unit operations | 2.4.1 | Complete necessary setting up, checks and adjustments |
| | 2.4.2 | Process batches of product |

Element 2.4.1: Complete necessary setting up, checks and adjustments

Performance criteria
(a) Specified PPE is worn and used correctly
(b) Materials are rechecked as being of the correct identity, quality and in the specified amounts at time of charging
(c) Materials and components are charged according to batch instructions
(d) Controls are set as necessary to produce product of the correct specification
(e) Specified tests are completed correctly at scheduled intervals
(f) Samples are taken as specified
(g) Statutory and site health, safety and environmental standards are met
(h) Records are accurate, legible and complete

Range
Operations: for batch operations and related tasks, involving several unit operations, *involving some problem solving, including some assembly of equipment*

Plant/equipment: moderately complex plant and equipment, with some control instrumentation, several interactions between items of equipment and people, and with a number of parameters within the operator's control

Evidence requirements
The candidate should:

- Demonstrate completing necessary setting up, checks and adjustments for at least one operation
- Describe how to complete necessary setting up, checks and adjustments when some problem solving is required and when equipment needs to be assembled

For all activities specified in the range the candidate should:

- Explain the consequences of incorrect charging of materials
- Explain the consequences of incorrect setting of controls
- Explain the consequences of incorrect or incomplete testing and sampling
- Describe the major health, safety and environmental hazards associated with this activity
- Explain the consequences of not keeping accurate and up to date records for this activity
- Describe the correct action to take on discovering defective materials/components

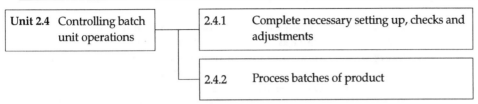

| Unit 2.4 Controlling batch unit operations | 2.4.1 | Complete necessary setting up, checks and adjustments |
| 2.4.2 | Process batches of product |

Element 2.4.2: Process batches of product

Performance criteria
(a) Batch operations are controlled within specified operating parameters
(b) Early signs towards deviations are analysed thoroughly and prompt action is taken to avoid the deviation
(c) Where significant deviation from the expected norms occur, appropriate action to minimize loss and damage is promptly taken
(d) Materials, products and waste are handled and stored in accordance with statutory and site health, safety and environmental procedures
(e) Accurate and up-to-date information about the task is made available to the appropriate people
(f) Equipment is operated safely without damage or unnecessary wear
(g) Work area is clear and tidy to the required degree
(h) Prescribed standards of personal hygiene are maintained
(i) Appropriate documentation contains complete, accurate and legible records of process data
(j) Operating procedures are followed at all times

Range

Operations: for batch operations and related tasks, involving several unit operations, *involving some problem solving*

Plant/equipment: moderately complex plant and equipment, with some control instrumentation, several interactions between items of equipment and people, and with a number of parameters within the operator's control

Corrective actions: adjust, request assistance, emergency shut down, *replace defective materials/components*

Evidence requirements
The candidate should:
• Demonstrate processing at least one batch
• Describe how to solve typical problems, request assistance and replace defective materials/components

For all activities specified in the range the candidate should:
• State the critical operating parameters for each unit operation
• Explain the consequences of deviation from each of the critical operating parameters
• Describe the correct action to take in the event of deviations from each of the critical operating parameters
• Explain why those corrective actions are required
• Describe early signs of common deviations
• Describe the major health, safety and environmental hazards associated with this activity
• Explain the consequences of not keeping accurate and up to date records for this activity
• Explain the consequences of not following GMP/GWP for this activity
• Describe the circumstances in which emergency shut down procedures should be initiated
• Describe the correct action to take on discovering defective materials/components

Figure 2.2   *Example unit of competence*

This chapter has emphasized the flexibility that the new framework introduces. Flexibility is obviously desirable, but there are inherent dangers which can lead to loss of quality. If everyone does their own thing, how can we be sure that the original aim of 'common standards leading to improved performance' is actually achieved?

Flexible arrangements must be set within a framework of quality control, requiring the establishment of the assessment framework with criteria for its operation. The new competence-based systems of assessment and accreditation supply that framework and criteria while the unit-based structure seeks to maintain flexibility, offer accessibility and choice and still maintain central control of the quality issues.

It is essential that training professionals understand this new quality-control mechanism. Readers in UK companies where NVQs or other competence based standards are being introduced should therefore ensure they read and understand Chapter 3 before putting competence-based training into practice within their own organizations.

US and Other Competency Models

This section briefly outlines what has been referred to as the 'USA model' (mainly because it was first developed in the USA, not because it is the only model used on that side of the Atlantic), and also considers the European view. There has been much exchange of ideas and research in recent years with practitioners utilizing the most relevant aspects of each system. Details of relevant reports and further materials are provided in the References section.

In the UK and USA, the impetus for change within the HRD systems came from the need for improved performance. Research into the means and methods to achieve such improvement led to the establishment of the competence-based systems which are now being used as the basis of learning and assessment.

Two differences between the UK and US systems are immediately apparent however. In the UK, the term 'competences' is used; in the USA, it is 'competencies'. This minor observation will often illustrate which system is in favour.

Secondly, the new UK standards or competences are combined to form units of *assessment of workplace activity*. In the USA, it is the use of competencies within the *learning* process that takes priority.

In both countries the focus has now shifted to the organizational arena and to in-company delivery (and therefore to the training professionals who work in-company). The private sector, attracted to the use of the new form of standards by the flexibility they provide, is expecting its training professionals to respond to the need for change.

In order to appreciate the differences between the UK and US systems, one must also recognize that there are major differences in the two education and training systems. These are outlined below.

Credit Accumulation

In the USA, a 'credit accumulation' system has been in operation for a considerable period. It operates more in line with the UK 'CATS' (Credit Accumulation and Transfer Scheme), which was administered by the CNAA (Council for National Academic Awards), than with the new UK system of National Vocational Qualifications.

Like the UK CATS scheme, US credit accumulation linked 'modules' or 'units' of learning to relevant learning programmes, usually degrees. Colleges such as Edison State in New Jersey maintain a database of 'credit ratings' for various learning programmes: each completed programme contributes 'credits' towards achievement of a degree.

For the UK, 'credit accumulation' refers to achievement of NVQ units of competence through assessment of actual workplace performance, not through completion of a learning programme.

A system of credit accumulation has also existed in Scotland for some time. Scotland was ahead of the rest of the UK in developing a modular accreditation system, having completely reviewed their educational provision under their 16+ Action Plan. Scotland has only one awarding body, Scotvec. Officers from Scotvec have been involved in all developments relating to England and Wales to ensure exchangeability between the two UK systems.

Qualifications Framework

Although the UK is developing a new form of qualification system, the USA and Europe are maintaining their existing systems, with some changes towards outcome-based standards in various countries. Movement towards the mutual recognition of qualifications across Europe continues, headed by CEDEFOP – the Centre for European Vocational Education and Training – on behalf of the EC. Readers who are interested in learning more of these developments can find details of relevant materials in the References section.

The European Perspective

Competence is also an issue in Europe. It was on the premise that the competence of individuals and the workforce as a whole was a key element in corporate competitiveness that the European Round Table established its Standing Working Group on Education in 1987. This working group undertook a study to explore and report on the situation and differences in education and training in Europe. It covered four levels: basic education, higher education, vocational education and training, and management education.

The working group's role was to evaluate the levels of competence achieved in present-day European HRD, to identify weaknesses and potential future demands. It was also charged with making recommendations for improvement.

One of the major recommendations of this working group was the need for all countries to consider learning as a 'lifelong process' – with the concomitant requirement that people are given opportunities to develop while at work. This has led to the exploration of practical models of work-related on-the-job training for technicians, engineers and other occupational staff – and of course to exploration of means of assessing performance.

Implications for Trainers

Use of the US model may well mean that training programmes are linked to a specific *programme of learning* (rather than a system of assessment as in the UK). For example, the competency programme of the American Management Association is a two- to four-year gradual programme designed to help managers acquire and use the 18 competencies in the programme model. Figure 2.3 illustrates this.

One of the first points for trainers to note therefore, when using competence-based systems in relation to qualifications, is that the UK model uses standards which are divorced from any specific programme of study, but are linked to a specified assessment model if being used for public certification. The US model uses standards which are usually incorporated into a specified programme of study; modules of the programme can be credit-rated to lead to public certification.

Of course, training does not have to be related to achievement of qualifications, but this is becoming more widely used. Incentives such as the tax remissions for NVQ-related training, and the degree-driven nature of US society add fuel to this fire.

For those trainers who work in international organizations, or in training centres, colleges or companies with European/international commitments, an awareness of the various developments in the competence-based field will be essential.

Questions of mobility of staff, including the use of trainers in a much broader context, become more urgent with the advent of the Single

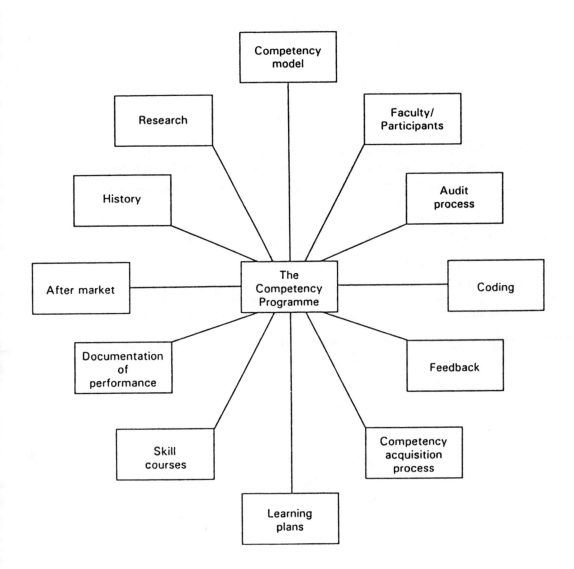

Figure 2.3 *The American Management Association Master of Management Degree Programme Competency Development Laboratory*

European Market. Trainers will need to be aware not only of the systems in use within their own countries, but also those operating elsewhere.

► **REVIEW** ◄

- Standards are now outcome-based, employment-led, independent of any training or learning programme, and based on work roles rather than job descriptions.

- Standards may form the basis of a qualification structure and associated credit accumulation system.

- UK/US systems differ in basic concepts but are not incompatible; you may wish to take the best from each.

- The European perspective is that learning is a lifelong process.

- The US system links competence-based training programmes to a specified programme of *learning;* the UK system uses competence-based standards as an independent structure for both training design and an assessment framework.

---

3 Starting with Standards

$\triangleright$ SUMMARY $\triangleleft$

This chapter will help you to:
- identify the standards on which to base your training programmes
- develop standards if national developments are not yet available.

Why Introduce Competence-Based Training?

As a trainer, you must be clear about the reasons behind the use of competence-based standards within your organization. Is your company/organization introducing competence-based systems:

- to make use of national standards?
- to introduce National Vocational Qualifications?
- to establish a company-specific competence system of performance management?
- to enhance flexibility of training?
- to raise the quality of training?
- to provide clear goals for learners?
- to evaluate training programmes?
- to assure quality within the organization?
- to develop/introduce a company qualification?
- to facilitate progression for individuals?
- to link with internal appraisal systems?
- to form a basis of credit transfer with formal qualifications?

- to facilitate selection and recruitment?

Within your own organization, you may find that any combination of the above reasons is relevant. However, if your programme design is to be relevant and effective, you must be sure of the role that training will play within the in-house competence-based system. The various approaches you need to be aware of are discussed in this chapter; whichever you finally choose, you will need to identify the standards on which your design will be based.

Standards – National or Company-Specific?

In the UK, national standards are developed across all sectors of all industries, and will eventually be available for use. If you plan to use outcome-based national competences, check whether standards are available for the occupational areas in which you are working. To do this, you will need to contact the Industry Lead Body (ILB) for the sector, unless you have access to the NCVQ database. (The database is available from the National Council for Vocational Qualifications. It lists all the standards which have been incorporated into approved NVQs.)

Where standards have been developed, but the NVQ framework and approvals have not yet been finalized, copies of the standards can sometimes be obtained from the relevant ILBs. ILBs are responsible for management of standards development within their sector. However, they are reluctant to release draft versions of national standards as the final published versions may differ quite drastically.

Should you wish to contact the relevant ILB, names and addresses are listed in the 'Standards Digest' available from the Training, Enterprise and Education Directorate of the Employment Department. Alternatively, check the latest copy of the 'NVQ Monitor', available from NCVQ's offices in London.

All national standards will be in a common format. Each standard consists of an element and its associated performance criteria, range statement, evidence requirements and assessment criteria. This can be quite a package (see for example Figures 2.2 and 3.1).

Standards are combined into units of competence, a number of which will constitute a National Vocational Qualification.

If standards are not yet available for the required occupational sector, you can develop 'interim standards', undertaking the analysis necessary to produce standards in the right format. This process is explained under 'functional analysis' (page 23).

This is the Key Role to which this unit and element of competence belongs.

This is the title and code number of the element of competence for this page; all the performance criteria and range indicators on this page relate to this element.

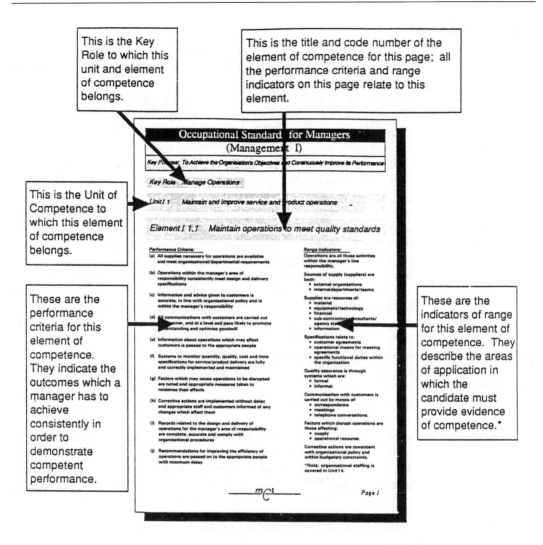

This is the Unit of Competence to which this element of competence belongs.

These are the performance criteria for this element of competence. They indicate the outcomes which a manager has to achieve consistently in order to demonstrate competent performance.

These are the indicators of range for this element of competence. They describe the areas of application in which the candidate must provide evidence of competence.*

*Consistent with its equal opportunities policy, MCI will make allowances where a manager experiences particular difficulties in meeting the full range due to disability.

Source: Management Charter Initiative (1990)

Figure 3.1 *Components of standards*

Company Standards

There are two options for establishing company-specific standards. National competence-based standards reflect expectations of performance in the workplace. Larger corporate organizations may wish to enhance or contextualize these standards to make them more explicit to their own needs. This can be done, but the format and the core of the national standards must be left unchanged if the company standards are intended to lead to national certification.

The second option for company-specific standards is to develop these in-house. There are certain advantages to this approach. Company-specific competences can be developed to meet the real needs of an organization, both in terms of format and content. If the development process is planned effectively then each competence developed can be directly related to business objectives. This allows the design of a system that can measure contribution to business success at individual employee, team, department or divisional level.

The type of competency framework developed will vary across companies (as it should if the development is tailored to aim for competitive advantage). Some examples of these tools follow in the next section. (For further help on deciding how to go about developing company-specific standards see Fletcher, 1997c.)

Making the Choice

After considering your company's objectives, you may decide simply to make use of national standards, or to enhance these with company-specific components – or to develop standards which are for your company only. However, if you are intending to use any form of these standards for the design of competence-based training, your approach must focus on *outcomes* and on the *performance* required of employees.

Developing Competences as a Basis for Training

Two major methodologies are used in this development process and are outlined below. The first, *functional analysis*, is used within the UK National Standards Programme. The second, DACUM, has been widely used in a range of analyses. A key criticism of this second approach is that it tends to be 'task-based' – it results in the definition of standards which describe the tasks people undertake rather than the expectations of competent performance.

Other methodologies may be used, such as repertory grid or critical path analysis. However, these tend to be supporting, rather than major, methods of analysis in current developments. Readers who would like further information on these techniques will find the References section of help.

As noted earlier, it is best to seek the support of someone with expertise in the field of standards development if you are planning a major analysis. You should check that your choice of support consultant is familiar with all relevant techniques and is able to advise you on the most appropriate method (or combination of methods) to meet your real needs.

Functional Analysis

This methodology may be used alone, or with other methods to develop the type of competency you wish to produce. Use of this methodology requires – but also generates – commitment and involvement from staff at all levels. While it demands initial investment, many companies have found that the added value of employee involvement has made this investment a wise one. See, for example, the case studies from Boots plc (page 74) and Whitbread plc (page 47).

I have broken the process down into eight stages, each of which is discussed below.

1. Complete occupational map
2. Identify expert groups
3. Brief expert groups and establish basis of groups' operation
4. Determine key purpose of
   (a) organization
   (b) occupational role
5. Apply rules of analysis
6. Establish draft standards
7. Consult role holders on draft standards
8. Define and agree final standards.

Stage 1: Complete Occupational Map

The term 'occupational role' is of importance here. Competence-based standards, particularly in the UK, are not related to specific jobs. For example, we might start our analysis with a group of individuals who operate within an administrative role – this might well include people in a wide range of actual 'jobs'. If we were dealing with particularly large groups of employees, we might narrow this down to a 'secretarial role' and involve, again, individuals who undertake a variety of jobs of a secretarial nature.

The first action in the development of standards, therefore, is to identify the occupational roles within your organisation. You might call this an 'occupational map'.

Consider this within your own organization – what are the key occupational roles of your company's workforce?

No doubt, when considering this, you had to think first of all of the key area of work – or key purpose – of your company. If you work in the retail sector, then the majority of staff within your organization may be in sales, or customer-service occupations. On the other hand, if you are in the engineering sector, a large number of your employees will operate in an engineering or technician role. Don't forget, however, that most organizations also have staff in what are called 'generic' occupational areas such as management, administration or training. Decide in which areas your standards development programme is to be conducted and then prioritize.

Your priorities for action will depend on a number of factors:

- your directives from senior management
- the purpose of standards development within your organization
- the number of employees within each occupational area.

Stage 2: Identify Expert Groups

Once you have your occupational map in place, you can begin to identify members of an expert working group for each occupational area. These should be 'role-holders', and therefore experts, in the particular occupational role to be explored. Your choice of participants should reflect those people who are involved in the full range of activities within the particular occupational role, and a range of experience.

Each participant will need to be available for at least one or two days initially, so you will need clearance for their attendance at a workshop, and for possible future workshops. (You can decide on these once you have the outcomes of the initial development work.) You will also need to make arrangements for the workshop including accommodation, refreshments and so on.

Stage 3: Brief Expert Groups

Once your group is identified, you can prepare the briefing notes or introductory section to the workshop. There are certain ground rules to be followed.

Misunderstandings easily occur because work on this new form of standard requires a shift in thinking. Remember, we usually think of standards as being tied to a particular programme of learning, or as something related to tasks, or as 'tolerances' or British Standards requirements. It is rare to find an organization where standards of *performance* have been made explicit; they are usually 'carried around in the head' – hence the 'sit by Nellie' approach to training.

Your expert group must therefore be very clear about its purpose and the proposed outcomes of the workshop. You might use explanations of concepts and principles from Chapter 2 of this book to help you in your briefing exercise. You must make sure that your group is aware of the following.

- The purpose of the activity is to develop competence-based standards – not training programmes or assessment systems.
- The standards to be developed are reflections of outcomes of work activity, not tasks.
- The process of functional analysis is iterative and flexible. As the analysis proceeds, changes will inevitably be made; individuals should therefore not feel defensive about suggesting such changes. They are there as the experts.
- The standards are a classification of the entire occupational area in which individuals operate and must follow rules of classification:
  - They must be complete, covering all roles that operate within the occupational area.
  - Each category identified must be different from all others.
  - They must have real credibility in the workplace.
  - They must reflect what actually happens in the workplace.

Stage 4: Determine Key Purpose of Organization and Occupational Role

When you have briefed your group, they are ready to start the functional analysis. This begins by establishing the *key purpose* of (a) the organization, and (b) the occupational role. Defining the key purpose of the organization ensures that the standards produced reflect the organizational objectives and not just the sectorally agreed benchmark of individual competent performance.

A key purpose is a 'functional definition' of the entire organization: we might refer to the company mission statement as a key purpose. If a mission statement exists, this can be used as your starting point; if not, you will have to establish one.

Keep in mind that it is the *functional* purpose we are looking for. It may be worth reminding you at this point of the difference between *functions* and *tasks*.

25

task	=	what is done
function	=	why it is done

Similarly, the *key purpose* of an occupational role will reflect the functional role that that occupation plays within the organization. Some examples of key purpose are given in Figure 3.2 (Training Agency, 1988–90).

Sectoral examples

Steel industry	Supply a range of iron and steel products by processing raw materials to meet anticipated and actual market requirements.
Training and development	Develop human potential to assist organizations and individuals achieve their objectives.
Retail sales (supermarket)	Make household goods available for sale to domestic customers.

Occupational role examples

Building society cashier	Provide financial advisory and direct investment services to individual and group (non-corporate) customers.
Manufacturing manager	Coordinate and manage human, material and capital resources and associated production systems in order to manufacture products which meet the needs of customers.

Figure 3.2 *Key purpose examples*

You will notice that all definitions of key purpose follow a set pattern. For example:

Active verb	*Object*	*Condition/Context*
Develop	human potential	to assist organizations...

You will also notice that the same statement can be applied to any and all levels within an occupation, for example:

The key purpose of the training and development sector...
The key purpose of each training and development organisation...
The key purpose of each training and development department...
The key purpose of training and development officers...
The key purpose of each individual training and development officer...

...is to develop human potential to assist organizations and individuals to achieve their objectives.

It is worth spending time on the definition of the key purpose. It is a critical aspect of the functional analysis process.

Stage 5: Apply Rules of Analysis

In whatever sector you are working, there will be a set of rules for analysis, often referred to as 'disaggregation rules'. We might think of these as criteria by which our analysis is undertaken. Some of them were included in stage 3 when the basis of the group's operation was established.

Disaggregation rules may vary according to the sector in which you are operating and will reflect the normal practice within that sector. In effect, they are types of classification. For example the rules might relate to:

- different methods which require different standards
- circular processes, such as the training cycle
- stages in a process or system – input, process, output
- distinct approaches or systems, ie those relating to people and those relating to products or processes.

This list is not exhaustive, and the type of rules adopted must be negotiated with occupational specialists to ensure that the most appropriate is adopted. A useful approach may be to brainstorm all the key activities, products, approaches, processes and so on within the occupational role under investigation. This will give you a clear idea of the range you are covering and highlight the best approach.

It is important to keep in mind the purpose of the workshop, however, it being very easy to get engrossed in a brainstorming activity which leads to a long list of items, only 40 per cent of which are relevant to standards of performance. Keep a clear focus on *outcomes* at all stages of analysis.

Apply the selected rules of analysis to the key purpose statement and to each resulting statement. By continually asking 'what has to be done to achieve this?', you will begin to focus on the actual functions rather than the task-based activities. No doubt there will be a tendency throughout the workshop for participants to revert to a discussion and definition of tasks. For example, if the group begins to identify a task such as 'type

KEY PURPOSE   Maintain and develop captive populations of exotic animals and contribute to the breeding viability of endangered species and the furtherance of zoological knowledge.

KEY WORK ROLES

Maintain and develop the zoo stock of animals	Contribute to the efficiency and effectiveness of the zoo within its operating context	Contribute to the research and development activities carried out by or through the zoo

Possible units

1. Maintain and develop the health of animals in captive conditions.
2. Maintain and develop the welfare of animals in captive conditions.
3. Maintain and develop the diversity and size of populations within the zoo.

KEY PURPOSE   Supply a range of iron and steel products by processing raw materials to meet anticipated and actual market requirements

KEY WORK ROLES

Manufacture strip materials by cold rolling processes	Manufacture small section products by cold rolling processes	Manufacture large section products by cold rolling processes

Possible units
1. Obtain and prepare raw materials for cold rolling
2. Cold roll materials to specification
3. Finish and pack cold rolled strip products
4. Contribute to the management and coordination of the production process.

Source: Training Agency (1990)

Figure 3.3 *Functional analysis to unit level*

letters', they are operating at too low a level of disaggregation. A typist or secretary does more than simply type letters – this is part of a broader function which might be expressed as 'produce typewritten documents'. This then reflects both *outcome* and function. (Outcome = document produced; function = production of (a range of) documents.

I have found that simply asking 'Why do you do that?' encourages people to focus on the particular level under discussion.

Continue to apply the rules of analysis to identify functions which will effectively form 'units of competence'. Then *stop* and review.

Units of competence
A unit of competence reflects an aspect of work activity which

- can be undertaken by one individual
- has real meaning as a 'marketable component' of work-based activity
- can be grouped with other units to form a credible qualification.

There is no precise definition of a unit of competence. Because it is the smallest component in an accreditation system, it must reflect a combination of workplace activities which are attractive to employers. Example units were given in Chapters 1 and 2. Figure 3.3 illustrates two functional analyses, taken to unit level.

Judging when you have reached unit level is something which many people find the most difficult part of the functional analysis process. As we noted earlier, the analysis itself is an iterative process: frequent changes are common. As a general guideline, when you feel you have identified units, as described in this section, first apply the checklist in Figure 3.5 (except points 4 and 5) to each unit; then continue with the next stage of establishing draft standards. Finally, apply the entire checklist to the completed units.

Once your analysis has reached unit level, your expert group is ready to identify occupational standards.

Stage 6: Establish Draft Standards

Occupational standards are comprised of elements, performance criteria and range statements (see Figure 3.4).

Working from unit level, your analysis will continue to identify the key outcomes of workplace activity. The example from the telecommunication services sector will illustrate the point. If you have a copy of the NCVQ database, you will be able to access this unit directly.

Install and Test Telecommunications Switching and Transmission Equipment – Level 2 (Draft)

Elements

- Prepare sites for installation and testing of switching and transmission equipment
- Position and mount telecommunications switching and transmission equipment
- Install links between equipment and to the network

Unit title
Assemble and connect telecommunications switching and transmission equipment

Performance criteria

- Site layout, condition and structure is safe for the work to proceed
- Site location and condition is suited to the operational requirements of the equipment being installed or tested
- Site is accessible and free from obstruction for the delivery and storage of material and other resources necessary for the work to proceed
- Specified plans, materials and equipment are available at the site according to schedule and stored in a safe and secure manner
- In cases where plans, material and equipment are not available the problem is accurately recorded and appropriate personnel are informed
- Potential disruption to the normal activities of the customer is identified and reported to the customer or the customer's nominated representative in sufficient time for disruption to be minimised
- A commencement, completion date and schedule is confirmed with customers and communicated to suppliers where appropriate
- Information is passed on to the customer or the customer's nominated representative in a manner that maintains and develops goodwill

Element title
Prepare sites for installation and testing of switching and transmission equipment

Range statement
Work sites – indoor, outdoor; above and below ground; industrial/commercial, military, domestic; new construction, modifications, extensions.
Customers – commercial, military, domestic.
Switching and transmission equipment – small-scale and medium-scale; radio, optical, metallic transmission equipment; analog and digital switches, power cables.

Source: NCVQ (1991)

Figure 3.4 *Elements, performance criteria and range statements*

Elements of competence

Elements of competence are the subdivisions into which the unit can be broken down: they are the unit's necessary constituent parts. The checklist in Figure 3.6 will help you to test each element you define.

1 Is the unit of sufficient size and scope to be recognized by an employer as 'marketable' – does it have credibility as a stand-alone achievement?
2 Is the unit expressed in language which is precise and consistent with normal usage within the occupational role?
3 Does the unit reflect a *function* rather than a task?
4 Does the unit contain standards (elements, performance criteria, range statement) which have a clear and logical relationship with each other?
5 Does the unit contain standards which reflect the *outcomes* of work activity?
6 Does the unit represent an activity which can be undertaken by one person?
7 Does the unit represent a function which is different from all other units in the same occupational role?
8 Will the unit combine logically with other units to reflect a complete picture of occupational roles?

Figure 3.5   *Checklist for units of competence*

– Does each element:
● use a language which is precise and consistent with normal usage?
● represent a distinct work function within the occupation?
● avoid describing procedures or methods, but focus on achievements and outcomes of activity?
● begin with a verb, contain an object and a conditional or contextual statement (where the latter is appropriate)?
● describe achievements which can be assessed?

– Do the elements as a group:
● identify, where appropriate, critical aspects of task or contingency management?

Figure 3.6   *Element checklist*

An analysis of the financial services unit ('Provide information and advice and promote services to customers ') would identify the following elements:

Element 1: Inform customers about products and services on request.

Element 2: Advise customers about non-FSA-inclusive products and services which meet their identified requirement.

Element 3: Promote the sale of additional products and services to existing customers.

Element 4: Promote the sale of products and services to potential cutomers.

Element 5: Ascertain customer details to determine eligibility for lending products.

Try applying the element checklist to this group of elements. You could also begin to consider the question of 'range' (see page 34). Our analysis uses rules which will allow for the full range of relevant workplace activity to be identified. In these elements, we have a range of products, a range of customers, and a range of services to consider.

Performance criteria

Once our elements of competence are defined, we can begin to define performance criteria for each one.

Performance criteria indicate the necessary *outcomes* of workplace activity. There is a specific pattern for the expression of these criteria: Each criterion should

begin with the outcome and follow with the qualities of that outcome.

I have found the following questions helpful when defining performance criteria.

1. What are the key (desired) outcomes of this activity (element)?
2. What are the key qualities of those outcomes?
3. What aspects of work organization, safety etc are critical to competent performance?

We can apply these questions to one of the elements within the financial services sector unit.

Element – Promote the sale of products and services to potential customers.

Q. What are the *key outcomes* of this element?
A. Information, and a satisfied customer.

Q. What are the *key qualities* of those outcomes?
A. Information – accurate, up to date, complete; options and alternatives offered, matched to customer need.
Customer treatment – polite, attentive, needs clearly identified.
Q. What aspects of *work organization*, safety, etc are critical to competent performance?
A. Goodwill of customer maintained; procedures followed.

You will probably find that your expert group has initial difficulty in focusing on *outcomes*. Early responses will relate to processes or procedures – they will tell you the series of steps they take in identifying the customer, identifying their needs and providing assistance. This is *not* what you are looking for. If you find your group getting stuck in this mode, ask:

- *What do you actually have? What have you achieved when you have done that?*

This will focus their minds on the final *outcome* of the workplace activity.

Once you have identified the outcomes and qualities, your next step is to express them in the correct format: always begin the expression of performance criteria with an outcome. In this way, your mind will always be focused on this key point. The structure and expression of performance criteria differ from all other aspects of competence-based standards.

Going back to our financial services sector example again, we can take one of the elements and look at the defined performance criteria.

Element – Promote the sale of products and services to potential customers.

Performance criteria:

(a) Appropriate and accurate information about the organization is offered.
(b) Potential customer needs and status are identified accurately and politely.
(c) Advantages and benefits of membership offered by the organization, are relevant to potential customer needs/status, are described accurately and clearly.
(d) Options and alternatives are offered where specific products and services do not directly match potential customer needs.
(e) Customers are offered the opportunity to make a purchase
(f) Potential customers are treated in a manner which promotes goodwill.

33

One important check for standards is that they must be assessable – there would be little point in having them otherwise.

The question is, how assessable are qualities such as politeness or goodwill? When dealing with interactive skills it is extremely difficult to pin down behaviours in a precise format. It is essential, however, that you attempt to express competence-based standards in as precise a form as possible, keeping in mind that no system will achieve the total removal of subjectivity. Within a competence-based system, training of assessors is of paramount importance, as is the quality assurance system which aims to maintain the quality of assessment (see Chapter 6).

We will not be going into great detail about competence-based assessment in this particular book: our focus is on the design of training programmes. However, you will need to keep this point in mind when developing standards and when building assessment methods and action plans into your training programme (see Chapter 5). The standards which result from your development activity can be used not only for the design of training, but also as the framework of both internal and public certification assessment schemes.

Range statements

Range statements define the situations and circumstances in which a competent individual would be expected to perform. Towards the end of 1990, and again in 1995, the NCVQ updated their criteria for approval of qualifications to include an increased emphasis on the content and format of range within the standards which form the basis of NVQs.

When defining range, you should always refer to the element title for your key focus. For example, if our element title was 'Arrange travel and accommodation' the range would relate to

- numbers and type of traveller
- modes of travel
- destinations
- health and insurance requirements
- travel documents
- monetary requirements.

Identification of range contributes towards the identification of the underpinning knowledge and understanding required for such competence performance.

A further example of a range statement is given in Figure 3.7.

Financial Services (Building societies) – Level 2

Elements

- **Set up new customer accounts**
- Amend and update accounts against instructions
- Process account statements on request
- Monitor the flow of cash into, and out of, accounts
- Identify, assess and action arrears in payments.

Unit title
Set up, monitor and maintain customer accounts

Performance criteria

- Internal/external documents are complete, accurate and legible, and delivered to the next stage in the process to schedule
- All signatures/authorisations are obtained to schedule and actioned promptly
- Correspondence to customer is accurate and complete, all necessary documents enclosed, and despatched promptly
- Correspondence to other branches of society and other organisations/professional agencies is accurate and complete, all necessary documents enclosed, and despatched promptly
- Cash transactions and financial documents are processed correctly and treated confidentially
- Computer inputs/outputs are accurate and complete
- On completing the setting up, the account is filed in the correct location
- Indicators of contingencies/problems are referred to an appropriate authority.

Element title
Set up new customer accounts

Range statement
Customer accounts:
Investment – notice accounts, non-notice accounts;
Lending – mortgages, further advances, personal secured loans, unsecured loans, credit cards.
(Note – requirements for procedures etc may differ in different parts of the UK)

Evidence specification
Performance evidence – over time for the full range of products and services covered. Simulations may be used as additional source of evidence.
Knowledge evidence – may be used to supplement that available from performance but as much of the work is proceduralised it will be difficult to make this effective. Knowledge of the different amounts is necessary in order for the candidate to be able to perform. Plus why there is the necessity for scheduling and the self-checking for accuracy etc; why all correspondence should be accurate and complete and long-term effects if it is not; to whom copies and correspondence relating to various products should be forwarded and reason for this (in terms of the interlinks between building societies and other professionals); why confidentiality should be maintained at all times; why indications of problems/unusual happenings should be referred on.

Figure 3.7 *Example of range statement*

Occupational standards in competence format are deliberately general – they apply across the sector and represent a benchmark of competent performance. Range statements, on the other hand, reflect current occupational activities and are therefore more specific. Two related sectors may have the same basic standards, as described in elements and performance criteria, but the range statements will differ, being specific to activity within each sector.

For example, consider the leather industry: factory production and the craft sector. Each uses different methods and equipment in addition to producing similar, but not identical, products. Some products are unique to each sector. The standards for these two sectors will therefore reflect both similarities and differences. Some units of competence will contain elements and performance criteria which apply in both sectors, but the *range* of activity (encompassing equipment, products etc) will differ within these units.

Range indicators

The term 'range indicators' is used in the development of cross-sectoral or generic standards for occupations such as management, or training and development. Because this type of standard applies across a wide range of industries, it is extremely difficult to define its specific range statements. Range indicators are therefore developed as broader guidelines which can be used by individual sectors as the basis for development of more specific range statements.

If you come across range indicators within a set of national standards, you should:

- check the status of the standards – are they in draft version? Are they cross-sectoral?
- seek advice from the relevant Industry Lead Body – have more specific range statements been developed?

You can, of course, use the range indicators as the basis of your own development process. Examples of standards using range indicators are given in Figure 3.8.

Identification of underpinning knowledge and understanding

The identification of range statements contributes to the identification of underpinning knowledge and understanding. If an individual can perform to the required standards, over the specified range of contexts, conditions, contingencies, etc then it is reasonable to judge that individual as 'competent'.

Competence-based developments are based on a 'broad view of competence'. This view includes the need for individuals to *apply*

Unit title – Manage operations

Element 2.1 – Contribute to the evaluation of proposed changes to services, products and systems.

Performance criteria

(a) Feedback from subordinates, customers and users is assessed and passed on, together with a reasoned evaluation to the appropriate people.

(b) Proposals for improvements are passed to the appropriate people with minimum delay.

(c) The advantages and disadvantages of introducing changes are assessed against current operational standards and the information forwarded to the appropriate people.

Range indicators

Proposed changes are received from and information fed back to
- immediate line manager
- specialists
- subordinates.

Feedback is gathered
- informally
- formally.

Proposed changes involve
- personnel requirements/team composition
- employment work practices
- nature and availability of services and products
- quality of services and products
- methods to reduce waste
- new equipment/technology
- work methods.

Change may have an impact on
- profitability
- productivity
- quality of service/product
- working conditions.

Source: Management Charter Initiative (1990)

Figure 3.8 *Example range indicators*

knowledge and understanding within their work role. It is important to recognize that it is not the knowledge and understanding themselves which are assessed within competence-based systems, but their *application within the workplace.*

There are two steps to the identification of underpinning knowledge and understanding. First, identify the range of activity: in what contexts, conditions does an individual undertake the element described? What contingencies does the individual have to deal with? Try asking 'What if...?'

Second, consider the *evidence* you would need to make a confident judgement about an individual's competent performance. Competence-based assessment is basically the collection of sufficient, valid evidence of competent performance. What evidence would tell you that the individual had applied relevant knowledge and understanding across the specified range of activities?

Evidence of competence

There are two types of evidence to be collected – performance evidence and knowledge evidence. Your standards descriptors should include examples of the types of evidence which might *realistically* be presented through *normal workplace activity*.

Evidence of competence is an assessment issue, but one you need to be aware of when designing training programmes. Evidence from activities undertaken as part of a training programme or experience can contribute towards the ongoing assessment of competent performance (see Chapter 5).

When you have completed all the above activities, you will have defined draft standards for a particular occupational role. Your final standards should look something like the examples in Figure 3.9.

Stages 7 and 8: Consult Role Holders/Define and Agree Final Standards

Once you have draft standards in place, these should be circulated to all role holders (or a large sample) with a simple questionnaire for completion. The key questions you need answered at this point are (for each element and unit):

- Does the unit/element make sense to users?
- Does the unit/element have real meaning in the workplace?
- Is the terminology easily understandable/normally used?
- Can the unit be assessed?
- Is the range statement
    too specific?
    too broad?
    complete/incomplete?
- Is the draft evidence
    realistic?
    complete/incomplete?
- Do the performance criteria reflect actual outcomes of work?
- Any further comments?

Production Machine Sewing – Level 2
Elements

- Create and maintain positive relationships with supervisory staff
- Create and maintain relationships with colleagues

Unit title

Create and maintain working relationships in a production environment

Element title

Create and maintain positive relationships with supervisory staff

Range statement

Supervisory staff who may be both familiar and unfamiliar to candidate in a social setting in which candidate has become familiar and where he/she is not expected to play a leading role in operating/maintaining group relationships.

Performance criteria

- Assistance is requested in a clear, polite manner
- Instruction or advice is responded to by an indication of understanding or request for clarification
- Verbal responses offered and/or actions taken in such a way as to satisfy for assistance, instructions or advice
- Disagreements conveyed in a tactful manner
- Responds to reasonable requests in positive, supportive manner.

Evidence specification

Performance evidence – See Assessment evidence guide

Reproduced by kind permission of Clothing & Allied Products Industry Training Board

Figure 3.9 *Examples of complete standards*

When you have received and collated the comments from this consultation process, you can continue with the standards-setting process outlined earlier in this chapter to modify and agree final standards.

You will probably find that the workshops and consultation generate considerable interest. This is a bonus to the development and also sets the scene for the involvement of all staff in the workplace assessment process (if this is to be introduced).

The complete functional analysis approach is illustrated in Figure 3.10.

With this work completed, you are now ready to use the explicit standards as the basis of your training design. The next chapter provides guidance on this next step.

DACUM

A second widely used approach to the definition of standards is called DACUM. The name derives from 'Developing a Curriculum'. Those of you who are familiar with NVQ developments will note that the word 'curriculum' in this terminology suggests that the approach is one which deals with inputs rather than outputs, and therefore that the approach is not appropriate to competence-based standards. In fact, there are many similarities between the use of DACUM and functional analysis. There are also two key differences: DACUM usually focuses on specific *job analysis* rather than *functions*, and the DACUM approach centres on the identification of *behaviours* rather than *outcomes*.

DACUM was originally used in a joint project undertaken by the Experimental Projects Branch of the Department of Manpower and Immigration in Canada and the General Learning Corporation of New York in the 1960s. It was successfully used for training needs analysis and training design in respect of occupational training programmes.

You may find the DACUM approach useful as a supplement to functional analysis or, in specific occupational areas, as a useful tool on its own. As with the use of functional analysis, it is best to obtain the services of someone who is competent in the use of this technique; again, you will need to identify a group of people who are knowledgeable about, (and preferably work in) the occupational role under consideration.

There are a number of similarities between DACUM and functional analysis. The DACUM approach involves the following steps.

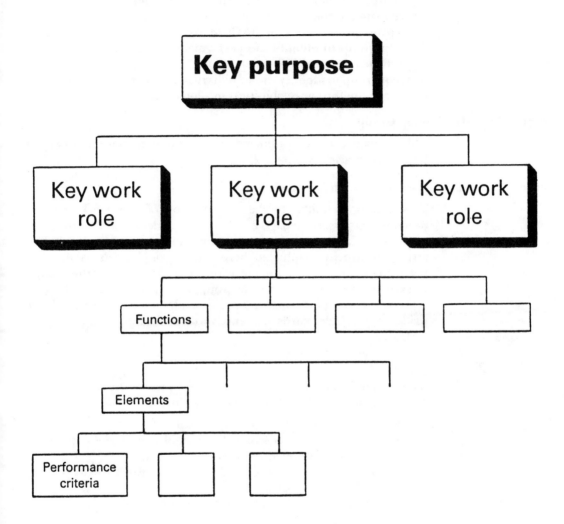

Figure 3.10 *The functional analysis approach*

1. Identify working group.
2. Conduct a review of 'key performance areas' for the occupational role.
3. Explain ground rules for DACUM to the group.
4. Help group to identify the performance objectives for each 'key performance area' (KPA).
5. Help group to identify the subsidiary performance objectives.
6. Arrange peformance objectives in a logical sequence.

Stage 1: Identify Working Group

This activity can be conducted in the same manner as that for functional analysis (see page 23).

Stage 2: Conduct a Review of Key Performance Areas

This activity is similar to the identification of 'key work roles' in functional analysis (see page 25). However, it does not have the same emphasis on a functional approach and can become task-based. This activity is usually conducted before the group meets as the 'key performance areas', or KPAs, provide a starting point for the group's work. You can, of course, get the group to work on this instead.

Once the key performance areas are identified, these should be written out on index cards, preferably with different colour coding for each area.

Stage 3: Explain Ground Rules

As with functional analysis, there are rules by which the activities must be undertaken. For DACUM, these are as follows:

- Comments must be objective and balanced.
- No response or decision is 'set in tablets of stone' – frequent change to developed work is quite normal.
- A key performance area is a description of work activity relating to effective performance.
- 'Performance objectives' constitute a breakdown of the specified job role.
- 'Training objectives' are statements which reflect the desired outcomes of training programmes.

Stages 4 to 6: Help Group to Define Objectives and Sequence them

The remaining activity within the DACUM approach is very similar to that used within functional analysis – but usually with a focus on jobs rather than functions.

The index cards with the key performance areas should be pinned to a large board, and the performance objectives relating to each one pinned beneath them. When the group feels that all the objectives have been correctly identified (incorporating any changes that have been agreed), the cards can be arranged in a logical sequence.

When conducting the DACUM activity, your focus should be on actual behaviours – what do individuals actually *do* when carrying out this key performance area? It is this focus which has led to criticism of the DACUM approach within NVQ-related competence-based developments, where this task-based view is seen as a narrow expectation of competence.

Combining the Two Methods

In my own work on the development of competence-based standards, I have found it helpful to draw from both methodologies and to combine them with others. Much depends upon the occupational area in which the development of standards is taking place, the complexity and level of the work role, the extent of underpinning knowledge required and the reasons for the definition of occupational standards. These aspects all influence the decision regarding choice of methodology.

The Information Technology Industry Lead Body (ITILB) specifically recommended that both functional analysis and DACUM were used in the standards development process for the information technology industry. In their summary of methodology (Training Agency, 1989) they outline their work as follows:

Clarify the project
Clarify the project ensuring in particular that you have a clear picture of the use of IT in the occupational area and of the job roles to which IT applies.

Carry out functional analysis
Convene a group of managers/supervisors or others who have an overview of the occupational area, its key purpose, main functions and how IT supports these. Carry out functional analysis of the constructive use of IT.

Develop preliminary elements and units of competence
Using the functional model as a basis, develop elements of competence. Group these into units.

43

Carry out task analysis

Convene a group of role holders who are experienced in the application of IT to their primary jobs. Carry out a DACUM task analysis of their constructive use of IT.

Fuse the results of functional and task analysis

Convene representatives (2–3) from each of the functional analysis and DACUM groups. Use the workshops to fuse the results of the previous ones. Review the developed elements and units of competence and identify possible performance criteria and range statements. Confirm the elements, units, performance criteria and range statements.

Verify the standards

Identify a wider sample of experts (usually about 30); get their agreement to take part in a postal questionnaire. Organize your units, elements, performance criteria and range statements into a questionnaire which tests your wider sample's level of agreement.

(The flowchart shown in Figure 3.11 may provide a useful guide for planning your own standards development workshop. In addition, the case studies which follow provide some realistic experience of the development and use of competence-based systems.)

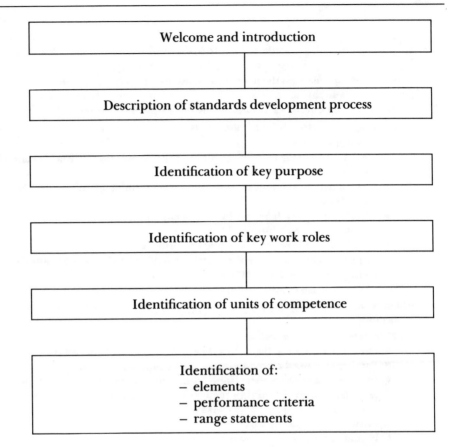

Figure 3.11 *Your NVQ standards development workshop*

► REVIEW ◄

This section summarizes the process of standards development and provides a checklist for your work in this area. It draws together all key points from Chapter 3 to give you a reference document for each stage of the development process.

Developing Competence-Based Standards

1 The occupational area

It is essential that a clear picture (or map) of the occupational area is established. Keep the following key points in mind.

- If you are not familiar with the occupational area, obtain the support of specialists.
- Clarify any specialisms within the occupational roles identified.
- Check variations within and between the target group of users.
- Consider issues relating to equal opportunities.
- Consider whether to use functional analysis alone, or to combine this with other methods such as DACUM.

2 The development workshops

Identify the expert groups who will participate in your standards development workshops.

2.1 Functional analysis workshops

- Participants should have varied backgrounds and experience.
- Participants need a broad view of the occupational area.
- Include managers/supervisors from selected occupational roles in the brief exercise, but avoid mixing managers and the staff they directly manage in the same workshop as this may cause some inhibition.
- Ensure participant availability.
- Prepare and issue briefing materials.
- No one should attend both functional analysis and DACUM (or other methodological) workshops.

2.2 The DACUM workshops

Identify participants using the following criteria:

- Occupational role holders should cover the full range of roles identified in initial occupational mapping.
- Ensure a range of experience and backgrounds.
- Avoid both supervisors/managers and staff in the same workshop.
- Ensure availability of participants.

Your Role as a Facilitator

Your main aims are:

- to brief participants fully
- to encourage full participation
- to achieve realistic, usable and understandable draft standards of performance
- to avoid imposing your own preconceptions.

Case Study: Whitbread Beer Company Cellar Service

The Cellar Service function within the Whitbread Beer Company has a three-year training programme underway to ensure that all staff are fully equipped to meet the challenges of the industry's future.

In 1990, the cellar service project team was set up, and established a shopping list of aims for the programme including:

- the definition and development of standards for all roles within the cellar service function;
- the design of an assessment process;
- the selection, training and development of two training technicians
- the training of all Cellar Service managers in competence-based assessment.

Explicit and measurable standards of performance were developed for each job role within the Cellar Service function. This included stores and administration staff and service technicians. All standards were developed by visits and/or workshops with the people who actually carried out the relevant role within Cellar Service.

The process of developing the standards, using functional analysis, ran along the following lines:

- workshop with delegates to set draft standards;
- circulation of those draft standards to all role holders for comment;
- modification and presentation to departmental managers for final approval.

Having defined and agreed the standards, each member of staff will receive on-job assessment from his or her manager – those managers having received training in competence-based assessment.

Once individual assessments are completed, and training needs identified, training packages will be constructed to bridge any knowledge and skill gaps. Everyone will continue to be assessed on a continuous basis, and will be able to achieve certification when they reach the required standards.

The standards were incorporated into units, and certification with City and Guilds was agreed.

Hence, Whitbread Cellar Service has a system which allows all staff to demonstrate their expertise and previous experience and to gain certification from a national body. This does not operate within an examination or 'special assessment' setting, where a test is passed or failed. The whole point of the project is to provide standards which staff can attain (at work) for the benefit of the customers and themselves.

Whitbread Cellar Service's expressed intention is to have the best-trained workforce within the brewing industry's technical services departments, and to recognize individual achievements by certification from a national body. They believe that this will achieve a number of positive goals, including the building of individual self-confidence and knowledge and a more positive approach to customers. The project also improves the ability of the department to provide higher standards of service and to raise the Cellar Service function profile within the company as well as in the industry as a whole.

Case Study: British Telecom

This case study focuses particularly on the development of in-company trainers.

Six years ago, all trainer training at British Telecom was based on the Certificate in Direct Training, awarded by the Institute of Training and Development. The core of this certificate was a two-week training foundation course.

Trainer development within British Telecom is the responsibility of the central training and development group. Initially, this was a small group with a large, internal, customer base. The demand for trainer training was diverse, with different customers needing different and sometimes shorter forms of training. This eventually led to a restructuring of the training department, each part dealing with a different aspect of trainer training.

This, in turn, led to nominally different categories of trainer and trainer training. For example, an 'accredited' category A trainer handled commercial training, a category C trainer management training and a category D trainer TQM training. The demands and complexities of this system created huge overlaps in provision.

In 1988, the training and development group was increased in size and began the development of the new trainer development programme, with the intention of training out of a common skill stock, thereafter training trainers skill by skill.

The decision to adopt a competence-based scheme was based on several factors, including:

- the need to train 'out of a common skill'
- the perceived benefits of a workplace accreditation scheme
- greater flexibility
- development targeted specifically to trainer needs.

Having tried and tested a category-based system, British Telecom favoured a system in which trainers who may only need to acquire an extra skill or two need not go through a whole new category of training.

Workplace accreditation was favoured because:

- the line manager is best placed to assess transfer of learning
- it fitted the 'zeitgeist' of new NVQ developments, etc
- the training and development group saw their role as one in which they would support trainers and line managers in the field when they wanted help.

The new trainer development programme is for training managers, trainers and managers of trainers. It is business-oriented and aims to develop the trainer skills that are required to respond to customer needs.

Each candidate for the new programme receives an orientation pack which contains:

- a guide to the trainer development programme
- definitions of trainer activities
- guidance on how to assess trainer training needs
- guidance on selecting and booking a training event

- guidance on roles of trainers, and trainers' line managers within the trainer development programme
- help and support available from the training and development group
- feedback form.

British Telecom's trainer development programme provides their trainers with the means to assess and develop their competence to carry out all aspects of the training cycle – needs analysis, design, delivery and evaluation of training. It divides the training cycle into 20 sections, 11 of which focus on the delivery function.

The programme utilizes a checklist to enable the individual and his or her line manager to assess current knowledge and skill. Sections in which current competence can be demonstrated can be accredited to the individual. Assessment against all relevant sections will reveal training needs.

Training needs are met by delivery of the relevant training modules: groups of activities which make sense within the working environment. Training is conducted by training and development group tutors who give feedback on each activity and highlight individual strengths, both in verbal and written form. Advice on further development is also given.

Individuals return to the workplace with a copy of the feedback provided. A copy is also provided to the individual's line manager who observes further workplace activity and supports further development. Line managers are responsible for ongoing assessment of performance.

Line managers themselves are supported by training in competence-based assessment. They also have access to a 'contact point' within the training and development group.

When national qualifications for trainers become available, British Telecom's trainer development programme will provide access to the new NVQs. Thus the organization will have a nationally accredited programme, but one which is also based upon and reflects the performance required to meet real business needs.

Implications of Change

British Telecom were quick to realize the absolute necessity of ensuring the reliability of competence-based assessment. If performance is to be assessed in the field by line managers, then there must be a support system which provides assessors with the skills and with the confidence necessary to maintain the required standards.

To meet this objective, BT are providing 'Training Manager Support Workshops' to bring line managers and training managers up to speed. The focus is on support, thus generating a similar approach within the workplace and encouraging line managers to give developmental feedback.

In-house trainers will be trained in the use of standards and in the design of competence-based training – this will be an essential part of their work when NVQs are introduced in other occupational areas within the organization.

Introducing NVQs and the more general use of competence-based standards across the organization is no simple task for BT. Some 30 lead bodies relate to the organization as a whole, including the Telecoms Vocational Standards Council. Issues relating to the identification and training of assessors, and the possible use of 'advisers' have to be addressed. Similarly, questions relating to 'ownership' may arise between line managers and assessors in terms of knowing the skills to be assessed.

Training programmes will be designed to meet specific needs. For example, activities within the trainer development programme will be combined to meet customer requirements and established against agreed evaluation criteria of quality and relevance.

The trainer development programme is now up and running, utilizing its 11 delivery and nine design activities in a flexible and consultative approach to the development of training staff. It is expected that the system will dovetail with new NVQs towards the end of 1991.

4 **Your Training Design**

┌──┐
▷   **SUMMARY**   ◁

This chapter will help you to use competence-based standards to:

- identify training needs
- design your training programmes/events
- identify the most appropriate and effective training methods
- consider issues relating to training delivery.
└──┘

Why Do You Design Training?

Few trainers actually consider this question in detail. We often consider the what or how; rarely the why.

Take a couple of minutes to come up with your own response. Make a few notes.

The reasons we design training may vary. You may have thought of some or all of the following:

- Meeting specified needs for development of employees.
- Providing training solutions to identified gaps in workplace performance or personal development.
- Meeting needs created by the introduction of new working practices, procedures or technology.
- Helping people cope with change.
- Providing solutions for performance problems.

- Introducing new people to the organization.
- Updating skills, information, performance within the organization.
- Meeting legal or safety requirements.

The reason for the design of each training programme or package of training and development may vary, but it needs to be clearly identified before design is undertaken.

As all experienced trainers will state, the initial research required to identify both the training need, *and the reason for that training need* is a crucial aspect of the design process. The lack of a real *reason* for training is what often leads to 'training for training's sake'. Training is not the *only* solution for difficulties associated with individual and group performance in the workplace.

Who Identifies Training Needs?

Training needs may be identified by a range of personnel within an organization – line managers, individuals, trainers themselves. Quite often it is a line manager (ideally through discussion with the individuals concerned), who will identify these needs.

The solution to these needs may also come from the line manager and/or the individual searching through a directory of in-company and external training and then requesting permission to attend. There is nothing wrong with this route in principle, although in practice it is probably not the most effective way to meet training needs since the support system required to make this method effective is usually not in place. For example, how do the individual, the manager and the trainer really know that:

- the needs identified are the real needs?
- the reason for the need has been clearly identified ie; is it really a training problem?
- the solution identified will really meet those needs?

Factors affecting this include:

- differing perceptions of the requirements of performance
- differing perceptions of the difficulties experienced, which affect individuals' performance
- how often in-company training programmes are updated
- to what extent (if at all) the trainer is consulted with regard to the training needs
- the relationship between the individual and the line manager.

All these aspects can have direct – and quite devastating – effects on the outcomes of the training function, though the first (differing perceptions of the requirements of performance) is perhaps of paramount importance. If there is a general lack of understanding or a misconception regarding the expected performance, other aspects affecting training design will only serve to exacerbate the problem.

The Competence-Based Approach

In the design of competence-based training, the likelihood of confusion or misconception regarding the expectations or requirements of performance is lessened. All personnel concerned with the management of performance (and therefore with the identification of training needs) have explicit standards of performance as a reference point for formal assessment and informal appraisal of individuals progress.

Trainers should be fully aware of the actual standards in use and the extent of their use. It is not possible to produce an effective training design unless the trainer, the trainee and the trainee's line manager all have a common understanding of the expectations of performance. This 'common understanding' is provided by the use of a clear competence framework. Trainers should therefore use this framework as a basis for discussions with line managers and potential trainees and for all aspects of needs analysis and design.

Taking the First Steps

(It is assumed that those reading this book already have experience in the training design field. Basic issues of design are not therefore covered in this chapter. Terminology used will be familiar to experienced trainers.)

The actual design process is not drastically different from accepted good practice within the training profession. An effective training programme (or any training and development event), should be based on clearly identified training needs. Its content should match those needs and provide opportunities for feedback and discussion. In addition, participants should be encouraged to practice and demonstrate skills and knowledge learned. Most of all, the training programme should lead to application of learning within the real-life working situation and have built-in evaluation methods to test its own effectiveness.

The first steps to be taken when designing a competence-based programme are as follows.

1. Review 'standards of performance' used within your own organization.
2. Review current practice for identification of training needs within your own organization.
3. Identify relevant competence-based standards (or develop your own if national standards are not available – see Chapter 3).
4. Check and match the competence-based standards, including unit content and structure, to the requirements for workplace performance within your organization.
5. Conduct training needs analysis to confirm both need and reason for training need.
6. Set framework for training programme.
7. Establish detailed content of training programme.
8. Decide on delivery methods.
9. Finalize resources, equipment and administrative arrangements.

Chapter 3 provided guidance on the identification and development of standards. The remainder of Chapter 4 deals with effective training needs analysis and programme design.

Defining Training Needs

There is little point in training people in areas in which they are already competent. The question is, how do we know that individuals and groups are competent in specific areas?

In a competence-based system, line managers and those with responsibility for managing assessment should be trained in the use of explicit standards of performance, and in the provision of regular feedback based on normal day-to-day workplace activity. If your organization has not yet (or is not planning to) introduce competence-based assessment, then your role in training needs analysis will be to undertake this task. This may be done for work roles, for jobs, for groups or for individuals.

Methods of Analysis

The method of analysis you choose will depend upon a number of factors:

- The size of the target group.
- The complexity of the work role.
- Time constraints.
- Your experience within the occupational role.
- The assessment/appraisal system in place.

Training programmes cannot be fully effective without initial research to establish a realistic and targeted design. For your research, consider what information is available to you:

- The standards of performance.
- Job descriptions.
- Interviews/meetings/workshops with job holders/managers.
- Performance reports (departmental/section).
- Self-assessment by prospective participants.

Desk research

If you have to conduct a desk research exercise (not a preferable, but sometimes a necessary approach), the standards will be your key source of information. However, it is best to supplement any paper exercise with interviews, or with formal meetings in order to identify both *what the training need is* and *for what reasons the particular training need has been identified.*

Training needs initially identified by line managers or by individuals themselves are not necessarily the correct ones. Check understanding on this issue. Training needs may arise because people are not being managed well, or are not being given information they need to conduct their work role effectively.

Meetings/Workshops/Interviews

If you can conduct a formal needs analysis, you might consider using the DACUM technique outlined on page 40. Alternatively, visits, meetings or workshops with the target group can be conducted. You will need to establish clear questions based on your early research into why the training need has arisen. The group may confirm or disprove these initial findings; they may also have completely different views on their individual and group training needs.

Delphi technique

Meetings or workshops take time; you might therefore consider distributing questionnaires to the target audience. Conducted on a formal basis this method is called DELPHI.

1. Identify the key training questions for which you need answers.

2. Select your survey group.
3. Brief your survey group and confirm confidentiality of responses.
4. Prepare your questionnaire format – keep it simple!
5. Distribute questionnaires.
6. Check that all responses are received.
7. Collate all responses.
8. Compile second questionnaire if necessary.
9. Distribute second questionnaire.
10. Check and collate responses.
11. Prepare and distribute further questionnaires as necessary.
12. Provide a summary report to your survey group.

DELPHI is a useful technique for use with a large population. If, for example, you are working on an organizational training plan and reviewing a number of work roles, interviews or formal meetings with groups would be impractical. DELPHI therefore provides a means to identify needs in a short time across a large target group. Make sure, however, that you phrase your questions clearly and unambiguously. Aim to achieve short answers and make sure you target relevant groups.

To be most effective, DELPHI should be used with statistical analysis and you should aim for at least an 80 per cent response level. If you are not at home with statistical work you may find that considerable time needs to be allocated to this approach.

Self-assessment

One of the most effective ways of identifying individual and group training needs is to provide the means of self-assessment. Competence-based standards provide a valuable tool for this process. Supply individuals with the relevant standards, together with basic guidance. If you can involve line managers in this process, this is even better.

Individuals and groups can discuss the standards with their line managers (and with you of course), or you could supply them in a workbook format, to help them develop their own training plan. Figure 4.1 illustrates how this process can be operated.

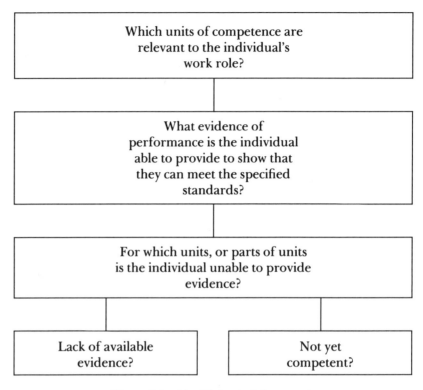

Figure 4.1 *Identifying training needs*

The unit structure of competence-based standards is particularly useful in this context. Individuals can be encouraged and supported to identify which units of competence are relevant to their own work role. The next step is to examine the units in more detail and to consider what evidence of performance the individuals might be able to provide to demonstrate that they are competent in each element.

Individuals (including line managers) will need support in considering this issue. Remember, 'evidence' can be of two main types: performance and knowledge. It can also be 'direct' (actual observation of performance, products produced) or 'indirect' (supporting evidence from colleagues, peers, customers etc). As individuals consider the evidence they might provide, certain gaps will emerge, where insufficient evidence can be provided. These gaps will be the training needs.

Your Training Framework

When you have established the units of competence which will form the basis of your training programme you are ready to put together the framework for your programme design. Remember, a unit of competence is a *unit of assessment*. A number of training modules may be required for each unit.

Use the checklist in Figure 4.2 to prepare your programme design:

- What do I want individuals to be able to *do* following this training programme? Will it cover *all* of each unit?
- Can I cover all the unit in one training programme?
- How many training sessions/modules will be needed to cover the content of this unit?
- At what depth do I need to cover this unit?
- What will I expect people to know at the end of this programme?
- In what ways will individuals apply the knowledge and understanding in the workplace?
- In what ways does the range statement influence the training design?
- How can I best assess progress during the programme?
- What are the best methods to combine training and assessment?
- What evidence of performance can be generated during training?
- What other units complement this one?

Figure 4.2 *Design checklist*

In considering these questions, you must have a clear understanding of the meaning of the standards and their application in the workplace. The most effective training is that which provides people with an action plan to take forward in the workplace. The results of your training programme should be *measurable*.

Training Content

A training programme should lead to an effective outcome. At the end of a competence-based training programme, you should expect participants to be able to *apply learning in the workplace*.

For example, if our element title is 'Provide feedback which enable groups to learn from their experience', we would expect that, following training, participants would be able to *do* this when they get back to the workplace.

Can the unit be covered in one training programme?

A unit of competence is a unit of *assessment* and incorporates various activities which, together, represent a complete work function. We also know that individuals can gain accreditation at a unit level. We need to consider whether one training programme will provide adequate support for individuals to learn and apply all that is necessary to achieve this unit.

Much depends upon our definition of 'training programme'. We could take this to mean a one-day workshop, or a two-week residential. Take a good look at each unit: What function does it cover? How many training modules/sessions would be needed to provide sufficient training and development? What is the current level of competence of your target group? Do you need to cover all aspects of the unit or only selected elements?

How many training sessions/modules? What depth?

When considering the number of sessions or modules (and therefore the length of your training programme), apply the checklist in Figure 4.3 to each unit.

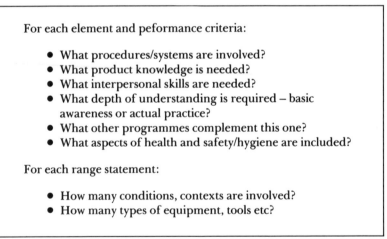

For each element and peformance criteria:

- What procedures/systems are involved?
- What product knowledge is needed?
- What interpersonal skills are needed?
- What depth of understanding is required – basic awareness or actual practice?
- What other programmes complement this one?
- What aspects of health and safety/hygiene are included?

For each range statement:

- How many conditions, contexts are involved?
- How many types of equipment, tools etc?

Figure 4.3 *Module checklist*

Using range statements

It is not *knowledge itself* but the *application of knowledge and understanding* which is of importance in performance-based (competence-based) standards. Therefore, in asking what people need to know, you are considering what aspects of performance require specific knowledge and understanding and how that knowledge needs to be applied across the specified *range of contexts, conditions or contingencies.*

Competent people can *transfer* their skills and knowledge across and between various contexts. The range information is your guide in the process of identifying which areas and what depth of knowledge you need to include in your programme.

Going back to our Travel example again (see page 34), you will recall that the Element title was 'Arrange travel and accommodation' and the range statement included:

- numbers and type of traveller
- modes of travel
- destinations
- health and insurance requirements
- travel documents
- monetary requirements.

Your training programme would need to cover all aspects of range in which training needs had been identified.

When you have considered all the questions relating to content, you have the framework on which to make decisions regarding the length of your proposed programme and the basic modular structure.

As with all good training practice, each module or session of training should follow a logical sequence. The focus of your programme should, however, be on the specific *outcomes* specified in the relevant standards. The combination of modules should cover the range of activity specified in the standards, matched against those identified in your needs analysis.

Training Methods

When your training content is clear, you can begin to consider the best methods of delivery. So far, we have talked only of training *programmes*; this suggests some form of formalized training delivery, but the approach is far from prescriptive.

Consider what the best approach will be, taking into account:

- operational constraints
  - availability of target group
  - availability of training premises
  - possible need for several programmes
  - atmosphere/noise at job location

61

- realistic activity: does the context of the work suggest that on-job development or off-job experience is more relevant?
- target group
  - what is their preferred learning style

Consider all methods available (and some new ones). The matrices in Figures 4.4 and 4.5 are useful tools.

Delivery Issues

The introduction of competence-based training requires restructuring of delivery mechanisms. For trainers, this means a complete review of current delivery arrangements.

For example, traditionally, colleges, business schools and training departments have delivered 'courses' – with set start dates, set periods of study and set assessment methods. A unit-based system of competence-based training requires not only that the course is broken down into modules which reflect the *unit* requirements, but also that the content of courses is completely revised. The emphasis is no longer on knowledge, or theory, or *what has to be learned*. The emphasis is very specifically on *what individuals should be able to do in the workplace*.

Competence-based training must therefore focus clearly on the application of learned skill and knowledge within the workplace setting. Training and learning programmes are unit-based and flexible delivery systems need to be established.

As individuals will be obtaining 'credit' towards a full qualification on a unit-by-unit basis, the demand for flexible unit-based training will increase. Some individuals will want to train/learn through open learning provision, some will prefer day-release programmes, others evening classes. If colleges and private providers are to meet these demands, both content and delivery will have to be completely reviewed.

For the in-company trainer the implications are very similar. The individual who may previously have been allocated a place on a 'full course' or to undertake the complete 'development programme' may now be allocated only to those parts of a programme which are of direct relevance to his or her needs. Flexible delivery and clearer targeting of response are therefore facilitated.

When planning your competence-based training, therefore, you must think in broader terms than 'the programme' – you must adopt an overview of the training function. The key points in Figure 4.6 serve as a helpful checklist for your training design.

Figure 4.4 *Training design matrix*

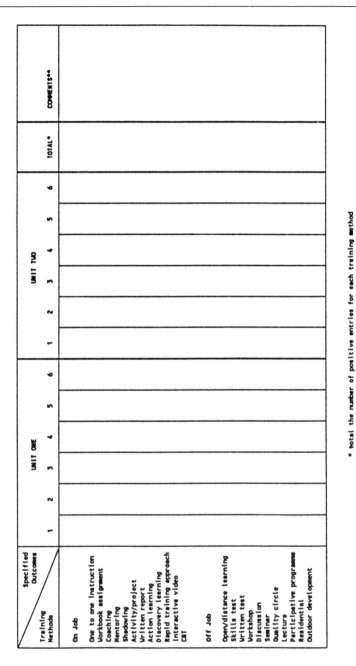

Figure 4.5   *Training method matrix*

- Who are my learners?
- In what working contexts do they operate?
- What am I aiming to achieve in my training design?
- How many units of competence are involved?
- Have I considered the relationship between number of units and number of training modules?
- Have I made adequate provision to cover the specified range statement?
- Have training needs been clearly identified?
- Who has identified these training needs?
- What delivery options have I considered?
- Do I have alternative delivery methods available to meet individual needs?
- How will my training programme be evaluated?
- What assessment opportunities have I built in to my programme?

Figure 4.6 *Training design checklist*

There is no reason to discard all your previous approaches to training design: the basics of putting together a training plan using competence-based standards are very similar to traditional approaches.

You will still prepare a lesson plan, you will still set training objectives, you will still make use of a variety of training methods – but you will do all of this using the explicit (and accessible) standards of performance as your base.

A Modular Design Approach

The following section illustrates how a modular library of competence-based training materials might be established and used in any organization. When planned and implemented by experienced trainers, who understand a competence-based approach, this modular system provides real flexibility and can achieve a cost-effective approach to training design and delivery. A modular approach allows for targeting of individual training to meet clearly identified needs – and avoids the 'sit through a week's programme' syndrome that so often occurs in a menu-driven approach. The following illustrations refer to 'units' (as would be used within a UK system). When using other forms of competence framework, the term 'clusters' or 'statements' will equally apply.

> **Modular Training**
>
> *Modular training* provides a flexible approach to both *design and delivery* of training and development.
>
> Based on *standards of performance*, each module represents a specific area of *skill*, or of *knowledge and understanding*.
>
> Where use of a wide range of equipment is the norm in the workplace, a single module can be developed to deal with *general maintenance, use, health and safety*, and specific modules can be designed for individual pieces of equipment or similar groups of equipment.

A Competence Based-Training Library

Development of the Library

The development of a competence-based training library begins with agreement of 'standards of competence' (competences or competencies). If these are defined in 'units' or 'clusters' a matrix can be established to relate developed modules to these collections of standards.

A module of competence-based training may be a short, formal programme, a lecture, a workplace instruction or one of many other forms of development. Once the skills, knowledge and understanding for each module have been defined, the relevance of this module across different competences can be plotted and a range of delivery methods recommended.

Modules should be clearly focused and preferably of short duration. In this way, maximum flexibility is maintained with modules being combined in endless variations to meet identified needs.

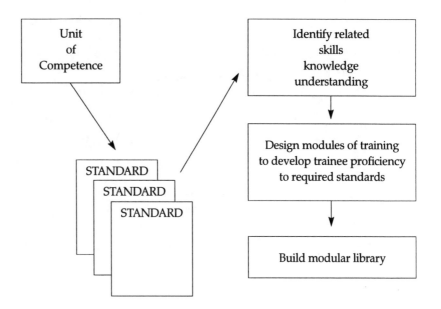

Combine modules into a programme to meet identified needs

Modules may be:

- A 5-minute workplace instruction
- A 2-hour (knowledge) lecture
- A simulation
- A half-day skills development workshop
- A one-hour drill
- A one-day practice session

To maintain flexibility in training design, modules should be clearly focused and of short duration

---

It is usually best to identify the 'core' skills and knowledge that apply across a range of 'units' or 'clusters'. For example, within an occupational area there will be specialist and generic competences. When developing training modules for roles within this occupation, the generic or 'core' modules should be developed first. By cross-referencing these to various roles, the basis of the modular library is established and duplication of effort is avoided. Specialist modules can then be developed.

Developing training modules

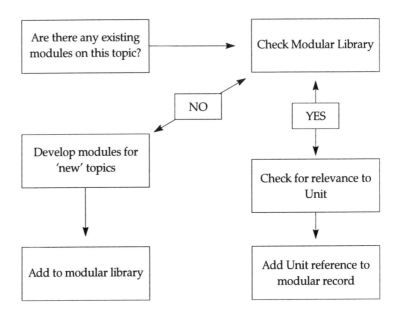

Using the library for delivery

There are now a number of software packages that can be used for a competence-based modular training library. These are useful tools for both development and delivery activities.

For delivery, a computerized database of modules will allow for a search facility by topic, or by reference to relevant competence statements (eg element, performance criteria and range in the UK or cluster/statement for other systems).

Identification of training needs is critical. If the competence framework is used for workplace assessment (as well as the design of training), then the full potential of the framework as a 'common language' is being utilized and the job of the trainer is much easier.

Once training needs are identified, the modular library can be searched for relevant modules and a programme constructed to meet those needs. In this way, trainees attend only that training which is relevant to their specific needs and training can be demonstrated as a *investment* rather than a cost.

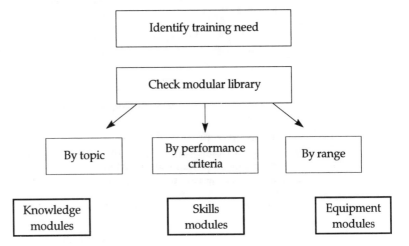

Selecting modules for training

Building in assessment

If competence-based training is to be effective, it should result in improved (ie competent) performance – performance which can be measured, using the same competencies as those used for the design of training.

Assessment should be built into the design of competence-based training – ensuring that one is clear on what is being assessed! Assessment within a training programme is *not* assessment of competent performance.

During, and at the end of a training programme, trainees will complete assessments which will indicate the *acquisition* of skills and knowledge. They may also undertake assessments during the programme which indicate *application* of skills and knowledge.

This distinction between *acquisition* and *application* is critical within a competence framework and is used as a development tool. Trainers must be clear on *what* is being assessed. Assessment of competent performance requires that assessment is undertaken in a realistic setting, where skills and knowledge are applied across the full range of specified contexts and conditions. While assessment within a training context may contribute towards assessment of performance, it cannot and should not replace assessment in a real-life setting.

What is being assessed?	
Training	*Assess proficiency:* Outcomes of training
Workplace	*Assess competence:* Performance in the workplace

Benefits of a modular training library

- avoids repetition of design
- provides flexible basis for preparing training programme
- facilities preparation of training targeted to individual and group needs
- allows for assessment of proficiency

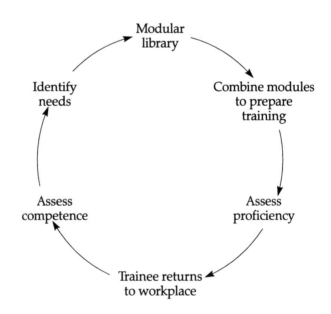

Summary

Competence-based training and its use requires a clear and common understanding of the concept of competence – whether this is occupational (workplace) performance, behavioural skills, learning objectives or personal skills.

The use of a competence framework as 'common language' for the design of training, assessment of performance and identification of training needs provides an integrated, flexible and cost-effective means of employee development and performance management.

The design of competence-based training must be carefully planned. A modular approach provides the greatest flexibility and avoids duplication of effort.

When introducing assessment within competence-based training, designers must be clear about the distinction between *acquisition* and *application* of skills and knowledge. This will ensure clarity on what is being assessed.

▶ REVIEW ◀

This chapter has focused on the actual training design, using explicit standards of performance as the basis. Key issues arising include:

● The 'first steps' to be taken when designing a competence-based programme:

1. Review 'standards of performance' used within your own organization.
2. Review current practice for identification of training needs within your own organization.
3. Identify relevant competence-based standards (or develop your own if national standards are not available – see Chapter 3).
4. Check and match the competence-based standards, including unit content and structure, to the requirements for workplace performance within your organization.
5. Conduct training needs analysis to confirm both need and reason for training need.
6. Set framework for training programme.
7. Establish detailed content of training programme.
8. Decide on delivery methods.
9. Finalize resources, equipment and administrative arrangements.

● The method of analysis you choose will depend upon a number of factors:

- the size of the target group;
- the complexity of the work role;
- time constraints;
- your experience within the occupational role;
- the assessment/appraisal system in place.

● For your research, consider what information is available to you:

- the standards of performance;
- job descriptions;
- interviews/meetings/workshops with job holders/managers;
- performance reports (departmental/section);
- self-assessment by prospective participants;

● In designing your programme, consider the following:

1. What do I want individuals to be able to *do* following this training programme? Will it cover all of each unit?
2. Can I cover all the unit in one training programme?
3. How many training sessions/modules will be needed to cover the content of this unit?

4. At what depth do I need to cover this unit?
5. What will I expect people to know at the end of this programme?
6. In what ways will individuals apply the knowledge and understanding in the workplace?
7. In what ways does the range statement influence the training design?
8. How can I best assess progress during the programme?
9. What are the best methods to combine training and assessment?
10. What evidence of performance can be generated during training?
11. What other units complement this one?

- You must have a clear understanding of the meaning of the standards and their application in the workplace. The most effective training is that which provides people with an action plan to take forward in the workplace.

Case Study: Boots the Chemist

Boots has been involved in the national standards programme since the earliest competence-based developments in 1985/6. The organization was quick to recognize that the perception of a national qualification is important for individuals and that the new form of competence-based qualifications offered opportunities for involvement of all staff in the employee development process.

Since introducing the Retail Certificate, Boots has found that enthusiasm and commitment to the standards-based approach have grown and has encouraged individuals to take responsibility for their own development.

Boots' training and development policy clearly outlines the roles and responsibilities for training, development and performance review. All line managers are accountable for the training, development and performance review of their staff. Training is provided by supervisors and store personnel and training officers. Line managers (ie supervisors) review performance.

Introduction of a Competence-Based Approach

Plans to introduce the Retail Certificate (levels I and II) initially derived from the organization's involvement in the development work of the National Retail Training Council (NRTC) – the lead body for the retail sector.

Issues to be considered included:

- How will the national competences match our own standards of performance?
- What are the long-term implications?
- How will our current training provision need to change?

Initial matching of competences and programme development was undertaken with the help of an external consultant and later checked with City and Guilds and the NRTC.

A review of current training and development provision was also undertaken. The existing 12-month induction programme was revised in terms of content, learning materials and methods to incorporate a much higher level of skills practice and competence assessment.

All training staff were provided with briefing on the principles and use of the competence-based approach, and plans to develop a new form of 'work-based assignment' were put under way.

The new assignments are modular in format, being available for all units within the Retail Certificate (levels I and II), with the exception of sales. Units for sales were incorporated into a newly developed programme.

Materials for the assignments have been prepared in written format. All new employees are started on the development programme and existing staff also have the opportunity to undertake the development programme if they wish. The booklets are issued by supervisors, who explain the programme and provide support. Once issued, the assignment booklets become the property of individuals who complete assignments at their own pace and review their work with their supervisor.

Currently, 2500 supervisors have been trained in competence-based assessment, together with 1000 countersigning officers. After training, assessors are registered with NRTC, but there are no plans as yet to certificate those operating in an assessment role.

Development by work-based assignment is supported by both on- and off-job training. There are now 18 assignments, accessible to all staff and available for use within any training programme.

New employees are registered with City and Guilds after three months' employment, although training is provided from day one. From registration onwards, employees are able to achieve unit certification. All induction programmes are now incorporated into the Boots Staff Development Programme, which includes a formal training plan. Each individual is given a file which contains details of the programme and documents for recording their individual training plan and assessment progress. Currently, 2700 employees are registered on the Retail Certificate and a further 900 are in their first three months of training.

As with many other organizations, the introduction of standards and competence-based training at Boots has not been without its particular difficulties.

One such difficulty often experienced is the relevance of all units within the NVQ structure to the operational context of the organization. For Boots, difficulties arose with the level I unit, 'mail handling'. Like many other retail providers, Boots plc found that this was not relevant to the actual work activity of its staff. A solution was found in the optional approach adopted by NRTC, making it possible to exclude this unit.

There are now plans to introduce the level III Retail Certificate and competence-based development for supervisors and managers. Similar, but not identical questions now arise – Will the Management Charter Initiative standards be relevant? How will they match with our internal competences? What quality assurance issues will arise?

Boots is very much aware that the introduction of competence-based systems requires commitment and investment and that a long-term approach is essential. They are committed to the approach, and perceive considerable benefits, both for the organization and for the individual employees arising from this decision. Not least of these is the flexibility offered by a competence-based system, together with the commitment and sense of involvement it generates within the workforce as a whole.

5 Assessment, Evaluation and Accreditation

▷	SUMMARY	◁

This final chapter provides a brief overview of three very broad issues which interact closely with competence-based training: assessment, evaluation and accreditation. Trainers need to be aware of the key principles involved in these aspects of competence-based developments.

Assessment

Within a competence-based system, assessment is the generation and collection of evidence of performance which can be matched to specified (and explicit) standards which reflect expectations of performance in the workplace.

There are two main forms of evidence collected:

- evidence of *performance*
- evidence of *underpinning knowledge and understanding*.

The *types* of evidence may vary and will include:

- *direct* evidence (products and items produced *by* the candidate)
- *indirect* evidence (supporting evidence and information *about* the candidate).

Evidence can be collected in a wide variety of settings. To a large extent, this will be determined by the *range statement* which is an integral part of the standards of performance. When a candidate for assessment is unable to generate evidence across the full range within the workplace, perhaps because of safety requirements or lack of opportunity, other means of obtaining evidence will be sought. One such means is the training environment: evidence generated during training events of all types can be collected by individuals and will contribute towards their overall assessment. Training programmes are therefore an ideal setting in which to generate *supporting* evidence of competence.

By building in practical exercises which result in products, (videos, tapes, completed paper exercises etc), your participants can take away real evidence which can be discussed with their line managers (assessors) and included in their on-going record of achievements. You might also consider providing a package for each module or programme which will include a copy of the standards on which the training module was designed: exercises, tasks, assignments completed and a tutors report.

When assessing evidence of performance, trained assessors will seek:

- validity;
- currency;
- authenticity;
- sufficiency.

When designing assessment within your training programme therefore, you too should keep these in mind. Your assessments should provide participants with evidence which:

- is *valid*—that is, it clearly relates directly to the relevant standards (an example of this would be a video of a counselling interview on a programme for the development of counselling skills);
- is *current* – that is, it matches the current specification of standards (a key point for you here is to make sure that the standards you use to design your programme are up to date: evidence of an activity completed well, but to out-of-date standards would not be acceptable);
- is *authentic* – that is, produced by the individual concerned (again, you need to keep in mind the need for individuals to demonstrate their *own* competence. Team activities will be useful development tools but it can be difficult to use evidence generated from these to demonstrate individual contributions and thus individual evidence);
- is *sufficient* – that is, enough evidence is collected to match elements, performance criteria and range. (Evidence from your

training programmes will contribute to the overall sufficiency of individuals' evidence collections. The primary form of evidence of competence comes from actual workplace performance. Evidence from training programmes can, however, supplement this, particularly in areas where opportunity to demonstrate a particular activity in the *range statement* is limited in the workplace.)

When designing your training, therefore, keep in mind that you can assist participants to generate high-quality evidence of performance or of underpinning knowledge and understanding which will help them to be successfully assessed as fully competent.

When building-in practical work, or assessment of progress, you should consider what forms of evidence this activity will generate and how such evidence will be matched to the standards on which your training event is based. Seek the advice of assessors and the participants themselves on this issue.

Evaluation

Training is only effective if it produces results. The key results of vocational training are improved performance and a more consistently effective workforce.

When designing your competence-based programme, you have an ideal forum in which to build an evaluation scheme. If you have completed the training needs analysis as suggested, you will have identified not only *what* training is needed, but *why* that training is needed. The 'why' should indicate the shortfall in performance. The next question is how you measure the performance after the training event to see if an improvement has taken place.

You may already have some form of training evaluation scheme operating within your organization. Check it carefully: does it actually evaluate individual and group performance back in the workplace? Or is it one which simply seeks information on how well the training event was organized and delivered?

Unfortunately, training evaluation is too often taken to mean the latter. While it is nice to know that the 'food was good' and that the 'accommodation was fine' and that the 'trainer did a good job', what really counts in the business world is 'has performance improved?'

Keep in mind the need to be clear about *measures* of performance – how was performance measured *prior* to your training event? How will it be measured *after*?

79

Competence-based standards, and the use of self-assessment workbooks and techniques are valuable tools to use in the evaluation arena.

Make sure you are clear about the techniques for measuring performance in your organization.

Accreditation

Within a competence-based system, accreditation refers to assessment of performance leading to recognition through award of a qualification.

Confusion is often caused when the word 'accreditation' is used in its more traditional sense, meaning recognition or approval of training resources. Outside the NVQ system, it is still possible to obtain 'accreditation' for training programmes, for assessment facilities or for both. It is hardly surprising, therefore that people have difficulty in finding their way through the 'accreditation' system, even if they are clear about their objectives.

Recognition of an Organization

The term 'accredited centre' may be used to indicate that an organization, which can be a company or a private training provider, or a college, is 'approved'. This usually means recognized as providing quality training. More recently it may mean that the organization is approved as an 'assessment centre'.

If your organization would like to become 'accredited' for either training or assessment, you should check with the relevant awarding body. More and more awarding bodies are moving away from approving training provision as the UK moves into a competence-based system. This is because the route, method or mode of training to *achieve* qualifications is becoming irrelevant. It is not *how people learn* or *by what route* which is important in a competence-based system, but *whether they can demonstrate competent performance*.

Traditionally, awarding bodies which approve training provision have been known as 'validating bodies'. This is because they validate or approve the training staff and resources as meeting specified quality criteria. These validating bodies have employed 'moderators' who visit the training sites to monitor training provision.

In a competence-based system, awarding bodies will provide 'verifiers' who visit approved *assessment sites* to monitor *assessment processes*.

The distinction between validating and verifying is an important one: it is the distinction between training provision and assessment provision.

Accredited Training Programmes

It may well be that your organization would like to gain 'accreditation' for its training programmes. This simply means that the in-company training programme is awarded a 'credit rating' towards a specified programme of study. (This is *not* part of the NVQ system but is often part of the academic award system.) You will recall that NVQs, and the units of which they are comprised, are units of assessment, and not units of training.

In the USA, this system of 'credit-rating' is well established. In the UK, it has been operating for some time. Most universities, for example, will accredit programmes which meet quality requirements. Should you wish your organization's training to receive such a credit-rating, you should investigate, with your local college or polytechnic, what courses would be relevant. These may include Certificate and Diploma in Management, and first degrees. If you decide that you want your training programme accredited (ie, credit rated), someone from the local college will visit and go through the detail of the programme with you. The course materials and structure will be examined by a 'review body' and a credit-rating awarded, if they decide that the course meets their standards.

When you take this route it is helpful if you first clarify the organizational objectives and the level at which this scheme is to operate. For example:

- Does the organization wish to have all training programmes accredited?
- Are the programmes involved vocational or academic?
- At what levels do the programmes operate:
  - craft?
  - technical?
  - first degree?
  - masters?
- Does the organization have any existing relationships with colleges, polytechnics or universities?

It is possible to gain national accreditation for an in-company programme (including full development programmes recognized as a full qualification) at any level of operation.

81

If you are not familiar with the operation of the education system, it is best to seek the support of a consultant with expertise in this field. You may find that your exploratory work leads you to negotiations with a wide range of educational and vocational bodies and it is very easy to become lost in the jargon and procedures!

▶   **REVIEW**   ◀

- **Competence-based standards form the structure for the design of training programmes and the framework for assessment.**

- **Evidence of performance generated during your training programmes can contribute to an individual's achievement records.**

- **Check your company's measures for evaluating training. Are there any? Do they measure improvement in performance?**

- **Competence-based standards and their associated assessment systems can form the basis of 'before and after' measures of individual performance.**

- **Clarify the terminology when thinking about 'accreditation' – is the objective to achieve 'assessment and certification' of competence, or to gain formal recognition (from an educational institution) for training programmes and/or resources?**

Glossary

Accreditation
The issue of formal recognition by a national awarding body that individuals have shown evidence of performance which meets specified standards.

Assessment
(competence-based)
Collection of evidence of performance by a variety of methods.

Awards
A general term for qualifications issued by examining or validating bodies ie certificates, diplomas etc.

Awarding body
An examining or validating body. In a competence-based system, an awarding body has central responsibility for the quality, but not the methods of assessment.

Competence
The ability to perform a particular activity to a prescribed standard. Competence is a wide concept which embodies the ability to transfer skills and knowledge to new situations within the occupational area. It encompasses organization and planning of work, innovation and coping with non-routine activities. It includes those qualities of personal effectiveness that are required in the workplace to deal with co-workers, managers and customers.

Continuous assessment
Assessment of competence on every occasion it is required during normal workplace activity. Used for formative assessment and to arrive at a cumulative judgement for final assessment purposes.

Credit accumulation
A system by which individuals can accumulate units of competence. When a specified combination of units has been achieved the individual can obtain a full NVQ.

Credit transfer
The acceptance of an award, or credits towards an award as credit towards another award.

Element of competence	The descriptors of the activities necessary for the completion of the function described in a unit of competence.
Formative assessment	Assessment during a course or over a period of workplace activity which collects evidence of performance.
Industry Lead Body	An organization comprised of industry, education and trades union representatives with formal responsibility for the development of national standards of occupational competence and a framework of National Vocational Qualifications.
Moderation	A process or procedure to align standards of assessment between different test papers, different testing occasions, different examiners, different centres etc.
National Vocational Qualification (NVQ)	A statement of competence defined by industry and based on nationally agreed standards of occupational competence.
Norm-referenced assessment	Assessment of an individual's ability in order to determine how well it compares with other individuals' abilities.
Performance criteria	Descriptors of required outcomes of workplace activities.
Range indicator	A broad statement of the contexts, contingencies, etc in which an individual must operate to demonstrate competent performance. Range indicators are modified to range statements (see below) within each occupational context.
Range statement	Descriptors of the limits within which performance to the identified standards is expected if an individual is to be deemed competent. Range describes competent workplace performance not the situations in which performance must be observed for assessment purposes.
Unit of competence	A descriptor of a discrete function carried out by an individual within an occupational area.
Underpinning skills and knowledge	The knowledge and skill necessary to perform to the standards identified by the performance criteria in the contexts identified in the range statement.

References and Further Reading

Black, H D and Dockrell, W B (1984) *Criterion Referenced Assessment in the Classroom*, Scottish Council for Research in Education, Edinburgh.

Boyatzis, R E (1982) *The Competent Manager*, Wiley, New York.

Constable, C J (1988) *Developing the Competent Manager in a UK Context: A Report for the Manpower Services Commission*, MSC, Sheffield.

CNAA (1984) *Developing Services Publication 6* (Access to Higher Education. Non-standards entry to CNAA First Degree and Dip HE Courses), CNAA, London.

European Round Table (1989) 'Education and European Competence: Report by the Standing Working Group on Education', *Training Officer*, February.

Fletcher, S (1993) *Quality and Competence*, Kogan Page, London.

Fletcher, S (1994) *NVQs, Standards and Competence: A Practical Guide for Employers, Managers and Trainers*, 2nd edn, Kogan Page, London.

Fletcher, S (1997a) *Designing Competence-Based Training*, 2nd edn, Practical Trainer Series, Kogan Page, London.

Fletcher, S (1997b) *NVQ Assessment: A Handbook for the Paperless Portfolio*, Kogan Page, London.

Fletcher, S (1997c) *Analysing Competence: Tools and Techniques*, Kogan Page, London.

Fletcher, S (1997d) *Competence and Organisational Change*, Kogan Page, London

Further Education Unit (1984) *Exploiting Experience: Recognising what has been learnt on the job as a starting point for retraining*, FEU, London.

HMSO, (1986) *Working Together, Education and Training* (White Paper Cmnd 2346), HMSO, London.

Management Charter Initiative (1990) *Occupational Standards for Managers*, MCL, London.

Mansfield, B and Matthews, D (1985) *Job Competence: A Description for Use in Vocational Education and Training*, FESC/ESF Core Skills Project, Bristol.

National Center for Research in Vocational Education (1983) *Occupational Adaptability and Transferable Skills*, NCRVE, Ohio State University.

NCVQ (1992a) *Criteria and Related Guidance*, NCVQ, London.

NCVQ (1992b) *Information Note 4* (November), NCVQ, London.

NCVQ (1995) *Criteria and Related Guidance*, NCVQ, London.

NCVQ (1996) *Assessment of NVQs*, NCVQ, London.

NCVQ (1996) *Implementing Standards for Assessment and Verification*, 2nd edn, NCVQ, London.

Training Agency (1989) *A Method for Developing Assessable Standards of Competence in the Constructive Use of IT*, Mainframe on behalf of the ITILB and Training Agency, Sheffield.

Training Agency (1988–90) *The Development of Assessable Standards of Occupational Competence* (Standards Methodology Unit Technical Advisory Notes), Training Agency, Sheffield.

Training Agency (1990a) *Knowledge and Competence: Current Issues in Training and Education*. Training Agency/COIC, Sheffield.

Training Agency (1990b) *Competence and Assessment Special Issue No. 1: The Analysis of Competence; Current Thought and Practice*, Training Agency, Sheffield.